TACOS

Desert Prep T4C4
****
09/27/2014
Andrew   7:32 PM
Tbl 140   1 of 1
Guests: 4

2 Sweet Corn
   W/ TACOS
2 Skirt Ap
2 Fish Ap
2 Chicken Ap
2 Lobster Ap

TACOS

RECIPES AND PROVOCATIONS

ALEX STUPAK AND JORDANA ROTHMAN

PHOTOGRAPHS BY EVAN SUNG

CLARKSON POTTER/PUBLISHERS

NEW YORK

Published in the United States by Clarkson Potter/
Publishers, an imprint of the Crown Publishing Group, a
division of Penguin Random House LLC, New York.
www.crownpublishing.com
www.clarksonpotter.com

CLARKSON POTTER is a trademark and POTTER
with colophon is a registered trademark of Penguin Random
House LLC.

Library of Congress Cataloging-in-Publication Data
Stupak, Alex.
Tacos: recipes and provocations / Alex Stupak and Jordana
Rothman; photographs by Evan Sung.—First edition.
Includes index.
1. Tacos. 2. Tortillas. 3. Cooking, Mexican. I. Rothman,
Jordana. II. Title.
TX836.S78 2015
641.84—dc23   2015006214

ISBN 978-0-553-44729-3
eBook ISBN 978-0-553-44730-9

Printed in China

Book and cover design by Marysarah Quinn
Cover photograph by Evan Sung

10 9 8 7 6 5 4 3 2 1

First Edition

FOR ALL THE MEXICAN COOKS ON BOTH SIDES OF THE BORDER
WITH RESPECT AND GRATITUDE

CONTENTS

RECIPES

PROVOCATIONS

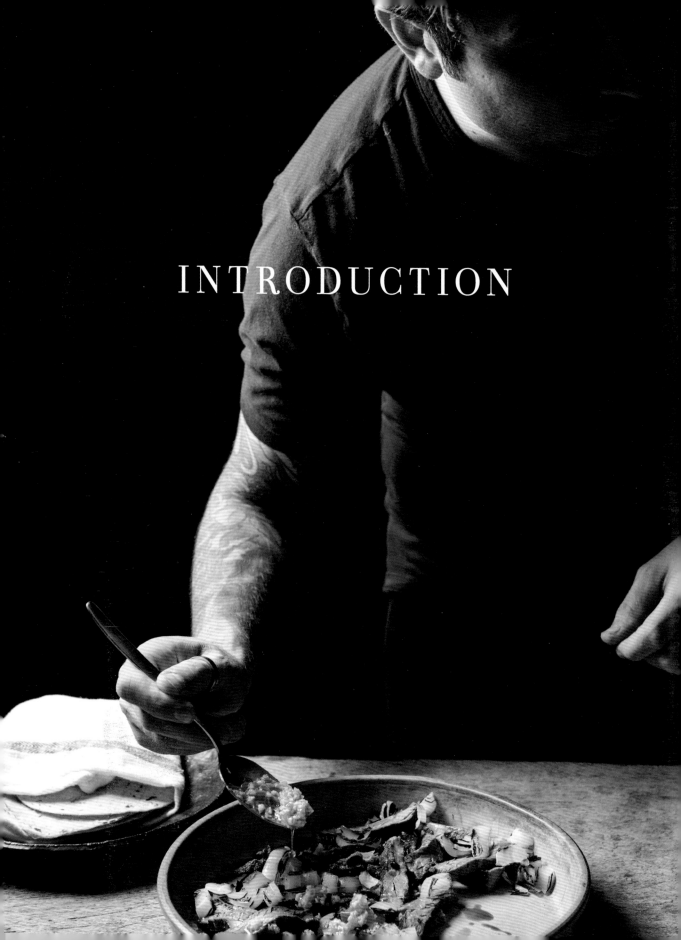

INTRODUCTION

Let's get this out of the way right up front. I'm a white boy from suburban Massachusetts where Old El Paso taco nights were mother's milk. I loved that stuff.

In fact, I wouldn't even consider Mexican food that didn't come with a spice pack and a sleeve of crispy shells until long after I'd graduated culinary school and settled into a kitchen trajectory that had nothing to do with tacos. In 2005, I was clocking ninety hours a week in the pastry kitchen at Alinea in Chicago. I'd fallen hard for methylcellulose and xanthan gum—staples of the modernist cuisine tool belt—and I regarded Albert Adrià's first pastry book, *Los Postres de el Bulli,* as sacred writ. The early days of Alinea were creatively grueling. And like a Dostoyevsky student who offsets all the Slavic gloom with a smutty beach read, I spent my downtime chasing a deliverance from haute cuisine.

I lived in a lousy walk-up in Lincoln Park with Lauren Resler, the woman who would eventually see fit to marry me, and on our days off she and I would explore the city's ethnic neighborhoods: the Polish Triangle along Milwaukee Avenue; Indo-Pak street food on the North Side; and— our favorites—the Mexican enclaves of Pilsen and Little Village. Along 26th Street, you couldn't walk five feet without tripping over a masa factory. We'd find ingredients there that were completely alien to us at the time: guaje seeds and spiny chayote, nopales, avocado leaves, and Oaxacan chiles. I'd bring this stuff home and comb through the index of *Rick Bayless's Mexican Kitchen* to figure out how to use it.

Cracking the country's cuisine soon became my off-the-clock obsession. Lauren's mother is Mexican and she'd grown up with some of these flavors, but we were going deep at home. We'd toast broken vermicelli in oil and cook it down in broth and chorizo for sopa seca de fideo. We'd pulverize tomatillo, cilantro, and serrano chiles into a bright green salsa verde and eat it with chilaquiles. We'd simmer black beans with epazote and chipotle, or stuff shredded chicken into a tamal de cazuela and bake it into a crusty, savory pie. We were mad for this stuff.

Then, on a visit to Los Angeles, I tasted my first real-deal tortilla and the earth moved just a little. We took a trip to La Parrilla, a taco place in East L.A. that opened in the late seventies. The decor was demented in the way only great taquerias are allowed to be demented: psychedelic mayhem with Mexican flag bric-a-brac, paper garlands, and Christmas lights dangling over sticky vinyl booths. But right there in the center of the dining room was the heart of the place. A comal—the flat griddle traditionally used to prepare tortillas—and a circle of cooks in frilly aprons tending it with the kind of calm, muscle-memory efficiency that tells you they've been at it for a lifetime. They would roll masa with their hands, flatten the balls into thin rounds in a tortilla press, and slide them onto the griddle. They would then scrape the tortillas from the comal and slip them, still hot, into cloth-lined baskets.

I've had three defining moments as a cook: the first time I got to touch a black truffle; the first time I made a stable foam; and the first time I tasted a freshly made tortilla at La Parrilla. It was elastic and gently blistered. Earthy and supple with the flavor of toasted corn. It tasted ancient. That tortilla got under my skin. And the more I learned about Mexican food, the more I sensed that what I loved about it didn't come from the same wellspring that makes things like nacho cheese Crunchwrap Supremes a cultural phenom in America.

A year later, I had moved to New York and was heading up pastry at Wylie Dufresne's legendary wd~50. The hallmarks of "molecular" food had begun to penetrate mainstream consciousness. Journalists called me daily looking for word on the latest gastro-trickery coming out of my corner of the kitchen. Investors called, too. It would have been easy enough to peel off from wd~50 and open my own temple of progressive cooking. But I knew if I piggybacked on the work of my mentors—guys like Wylie, Grant Achatz, and Ken Oringer at Boston's Clio, where I began my career—I'd see it as a personal failure. I wouldn't have made a statement, wouldn't have ruffled any feathers. I needed to do something provocative.

I thought back to those days I spent experimenting with chiles in Chicago. I thought of how much I liked that world, and of how challenging it would be to course-correct at this point in my career—to go from pastry to savory, to take a deep dive from modernist fine dining into the traditions of Mexican cooking. But I've never been interested in being reasonable. That's no fun. So I left wd~50 and began hatching plans to open a taqueria. My peers scratched their heads at what seemed like a professional reversal. I explained I wanted to cut off one arm to force myself to learn to use the other. But it would be a while before I got the hang of it.

Empellón Taqueria opened on March 21, 2011. I remember it as the day I realized I had no idea what the hell I was doing. I thought tacos would be an easy entry point for me as a chef: a tortilla, some salsa, a filling. Simple enough, until the first night of service arrived and the complexity of a well-made taco became maddeningly clear. All at once, I understood that the life span of a warm tortilla is stupidly brief—that making sure a taco arrives at the table with some fight left in it is a sophisticated orchestration of timing and planning; that I was not at all prepared for this. We were slammed with mile-long tickets: 19 tacos for a four-top, each requiring its own, intricate prep. The tortilla station couldn't keep up, and we were instantly in the weeds. I had invited my father and a journalist to join us in the kitchen on opening night, and both of them looked on in abject horror as we went down in a blaze of expletives. Tacos, man. Who knew?

In the years since, we pulled it together. We opened two additional restaurants—Empellón Cocina and Empellón Al Pastor, in New York's East Village—and a million tacos later, I'm finally approaching terra firma. In Spanish, "empellón" means "push." In my restaurants, we use the word as a war cry to get through a busy service. But my imperative to push extends beyond the kitchen. I want to push through stale ideas about what Mexican food is or needs to be; to push through the impulse to simplify foreign recipes until they are no more threatening than a ham sandwich. I want to push through my own instincts to beautify a cuisine that isn't concerned with looking pretty; to push through uncomfortable conversations about what it means to be a white male cooking Mexican food in America; to push until you can see why vanguard recipes should live alongside classic ones.

Push. There's good stuff on the other side.

THE UNITED STATES OF
MEXICO

Americans and Mexican food. What a weird, twisted love affair. To understand it, you have to dig deep—into the complicated politics of shared borders and migration patterns; into the needle-work of American cuisine; into our tendency to dismantle foreign things and remake them in our own image. And certainly into the knotty relationship we have with the Mexican nation itself.

We love Mexico for its beaches, ancient ruins, and natural wonders. But we also count on it for uglier things. For cheap Oxycontin and paradita girls. For Spring Break she-nanigans and border-town indiscretions. For the billions of dollars of cocaine trafficked through the country that we wag at with one finger and rub into our gums with another. Cheap thrills.

Maybe you don't see yourself in any of that. Maybe you've never been to Mexico. But if you live in America, you depend on Mexico's resources, especially when it comes to what you eat. Mexico is America's third-largest trading partner. In 2013, we spent more than $17 billion importing food alone—particularly fresh fruits and vegetables. Mexicans grow our food, and in many, if not most, professional kitchens in the United States, they cook it for us, too. They wash the dishes we eat it off of. The restaurant industry loves its superstar chefs, but that industry is fueled by Mexican labor on both sides of the border.

But what does all of this sociopolitical prattle have to do with tacos? A lot, in my opinion. Our proximity to Mexico means that, over time, its cuisine has become famil-iar; we've taken a kind of ownership of it. The lines separating Mexican cuisine from Ameri-can regional Tex-Mex are so blurred that a lot of us don't even distinguish the difference. In chain restaurants throughout the United States, Mexican food looks like birthday som-breros, nachos, and neon margaritas erupt-ing from a slushy machine. In cities like Los Angeles and San Francisco, Mexican food can look like fish tacos or chubby Mission burri-tos. In Houston or San Antonio, it might be chile con carne or "puffy tacos." However it manifests, though, that "cheap thrills" atti-tude extends to the way we think of Mexican food. It can seem as if there's a glass ceiling that caps the cuisine in America: we know what it should look like (saucy and cheesy), and we know what it should cost (not much).

Even in sophisticated "foodie" circles, Mexican cuisine sees its quality measured by how well it adheres to some myth of authen-ticity. That's a losing proposition, of course. What someone from Southern California views as authentic Mexican food differs wildly from someone who grew up on versions of it in Texas or, for that matter, in Veracruz or Puebla. The idea that authenticity is a fixed and rigid thing is absurd for a food culture that has gone through as much historic change and reinvention as Mexican gastronomy. It is itself a fusion cuisine, after all. What we identify as Mexican is actually a kaleidoscopic blend of indigenous Mesoamerican crops and traditions with the fruits of Spanish colonization: dairy, pork, and poultry; distillation; even the technique of frying is said to have arrived on Mexican shores courtesy of the conquistadors.

To declare that the only good Mexican food is "authentic" Mexican food also assumes that the cuisine has ceased evolving. No one tells Daniel Boulud his food is not French because there is vadouvan curry on his langoustines or turmeric on his veal. Like so many international cuisines, Mexican food has thrived as it has adapted, and it isn't done doing that. In a global market, evolution can happen anywhere: in the food stalls of Oaxaca, in the new wave of fine-dining restaurants of Mexico City, in my kitchens in New York, or in the pages of this book.

Read this book, and you'll learn some fundamentals, starting with everything I know about tortillas: the journey they take from corn kernel to griddle, why it's so important to eat them at their freshest, and even how to manipulate them with nontraditional ingredients. You'll gain a deep arsenal of salsas: simple ones that come together with a few raw ingredients, and complex ones that deepen in flavor as they simmer, perfuming your kitchen with toasted spices and chiles.

And, of course, you'll learn to prepare taco fillings. Some are classic, like sticky pork carnitas, musky tripe, or cochinita pibil (the last a slow-roasted pork that I'll show you how to cook in both a conventional oven and a backyard fire pit). Other tacos here use tradition as a springboard for innovation or as an opportunity to explore my own roots in a Mexican context. To that end, there are oyster tacos that give a nod to the seafood shacks of my native New England, foam-topped tacos that remind me of my days working in modernist kitchens, and haute cuisine tacos that articulate my belief that Mexican food need not always be cheap.

But don't forget as you read this book that I'm an outsider in this space. I, too, grew up eating crispy shells stuffed with ground beef and shredded cheddar. A lot of us did, and that's exactly why this book is not a sweeping study of Mexican culinary traditions. It is *only* about tacos—a reference point most of us share, a familiar food that we can use to explore unfamiliar flavors and challenging ideas. Talking about tacos gives us a chance to talk about cultural exchange, about idea appropriation, and about the way we value—or undervalue—ethnic cuisines.

That's really what's happening in these pages: We're using the taco as a Trojan horse. And it's time to open the gates.

GUAJE SEEDS

THE MEXICAN PANTRY

Chiles, herbs, and other things I want to talk about

ACHIOTE

Achiote is a tropical shrub that produces a spiny, inedible fruit with rusty orange seeds. Known as annatto in most parts of the world, those seeds are often used as a natural colorant, especially for cheeses like cheddar and mimo-lette. But in Mexican gastronomy, achiote plays a more central role, adding complex, bitter, and earthy flavor to seasoning pastes common in Oaxaca and the Yucatán.

AVOCADO AND AVOCADO LEAVES

There are countless varieties of avocado grown in Mexico, but only a few within reach here broadly in the United States. The black, pebbly-skinned Haas avocado is ideal. Avoid the big, green Florida avocados—they are watery and have an inferior texture, and their large size will throw off the recipes in this book. When garnishing a taco with avocado, cut lengthwise spears; if you're making guaca-mole, mash the fruit gently so that you can see a gradient of color.

In this book, I also call for the leaves of the avocado plant. The anise-flavored fronds are similar to bay leaves and are used, among other applications, to perfume Oaxacan lamb barbacoa. But if you have a buddy who grows avocado trees, don't assume you can use those leaves. Most avocado leaves are toxic, and the dried, aromatic ones come from a specific variety. Stick to what's sold by a spice purveyor.

CANELA

Most of the cinnamon we consume in the United States is actually cassia, one species of the aromatic bark. True cinnamon—*Cinnamomum verum*—comes from a different tree altogether. It is commonly called Ceylon, a reference to the South Asian island to which the tree is native (now known as Sri Lanka). But in Mexico, and thus in this book, it's called canela. Canela quills are softer and flakier than cassia and the flavor is more mellow, which makes it play well in savory dishes. If you're stocking a Mexican pantry and have both canela and piloncillo (see page 18) on hand, you can make café de olla—dark-roast coffee grounds steeped in spiced sugar syrup.

CHIHUAHUA CHEESE

This ubiquitous soft and mild cow's-milk cheese melts beau-tifully, so it is ideal for queso fundido, chiles rellenos, and que-sadillas. If you have a difficult time finding it, you can substitute jack or a mild white cheddar.

COTIJA CHEESE

Named after the town of Cotija in Michoacán, this cow's-milk cheese is hard and crumbly, like a Mexican Parmesan. It is one of the saltiest cheeses around, rivaling feta in its intensity.

EPAZOTE

Epazote is one of those staples of the Mexican pantry that never quite crossed over in America. The spiky leaves and tightly clustered flowers provide a pungent, slight anise flavor and an aroma that's a little bit like turpentine. So, yeah, epazote is an acquired taste. But it's also one of the most prevalent herbs in Mexican cooking, and loving the cuisine means learn-ing to love all of the little details that make it sing. You can buy it in Mexican grocery stores, and it's also quite easy to grow. You can usually find dried epazote in the same section of the market that stocks dried chiles. Party trivia: epazote is a carminative—it helps keep gas from forming in the gas-trointestinal tract—which is why it is so commonly paired with beans.

GUAJE SEEDS

Leucaena tree pods look a little bit like overgrown snow peas: flat and slender with seeds that are visible through the flesh. Those seeds are known as guajes, and they taste grassy, garlicky, and a little like the spawn of a pumpkin and a sesame seed. The kernels can be eaten raw or toasted, and are often ground and used to thicken sauces. Guajes are an easy find in a Mexican grocer but quite difficult to find in a gringo one. When shopping for fresh guajes, look for ones that appear fresh and unblemished. You might also encounter red guaje pods, but they yield the same green seeds. To free the seeds, slit the pods up the side with a paring knife and pry them apart.

HOJA SANTA

Many people associate the peculiar flavor of this large-leafed herb with sassafras—so much so that it is often marketed in the United States as a "root beer plant." In Mexican cuisine, however, it is used in savory preparations. Hoja santa is an important flavor in Oaxacan Mole Verde and it is also utilized as a wrapper for traditional black bean tamales.

KOSHER SALT

The two most common brands of kosher salt—Diamond Crystal and Morton's—vary in their density. That's a fancy way of saying that they have different flake sizes, so a teaspoon of one will be saltier than the same measurement of the other. (Morton's is much denser, and therefore tastes more salty.) With the exception of a few recipes that also call for flaky Maldon salt, I exclusively used Diamond Crystal in this book; use whatever you have on hand, but be sure to taste and adjust the seasoning as you cook.

LARD

Rendered pork fat—manteca de cerdo—is our preferred cooking fat throughout this book. Lard has a relatively high smoke point so it is ideal for frying, and it provides a richness, dimension, and distinctly Mexican flavor that you just can't replicate using other fats. Still, because so many of the recipes in this book are vegetarian-friendly, I've made allowances to give you the option of keeping a dish meatless. Vegetable oil is a fine substitute, but to paraphrase Maslow's hierarchy of needs, if you can use lard, you must use lard.

LEAFY HERBS

Of all the recipe conventions in this book, the way I chose to list leafy herbs is probably the most annoying. I'm fully aware that counting leaves is tedious and fussy work, but it's the closest way to get an accurate measurement without using a scale. Bunch sizes vary and listing a "packed cup" is problematic, too: who is packing it, and how hard? I've provided sprig count estimates throughout to make it easier to eyeball the quantities needed. Generally the guideline looks like this: 1 cilantro sprig yields about 4 leaves; 1 mint sprig yields about 6 leaves; 1 parsley sprig yields about 5 leaves; and 1 epazote branch yields about 6 leaves.

MEXICAN OREGANO

When I talk about oregano in this book, I am not talking about the stuff you sprinkle on your pizza. There are two types of oregano available. The first and most familiar is Mediterranean oregano, a peppery seasoning related to marjoram and native to countries like Italy, Greece, and Spain. Mexican oregano is an entirely different plant: a botanical cousin of lemon verbena, it tastes citrusy with a bit of tarragon licorice flavor. You can find dried Mexican oregano at a Mexican grocery, online, or at specialty retailers such as Williams-Sonoma.

PILONCILLO

Unrefined cane sugar—cane juice that is reduced to a syrup and then hardened—is a common sweetener that goes by a lot of names in Latin America. In Mexico, it is called piloncillo, and it is sold in dense, stout cones that offer a rummy molasses flavor unmatched by American brown sugar. Piloncillo is fairly easy to find in specialty grocers or online. Note that it is much more solid than standard brown sugar; you should break it up with a sharp knife before adding it to a blender or food processor. Exposed cones can be stored in an airtight container in your spice cupboard.

QUESO FRESCO

Also sometimes called queso blanco, queso fresco is a fresh white cheese made from either cow's or goat's milk. As cheeses go, this one is very simple: It's just boiled milk treated with acid (rather than rennet) to set the curds; the curds are then collected and drained in cheesecloth. Most tacos benefit from a creamy sprinkle of queso fresco.

QUESILLO

This cow's-milk cheese—also sometimes known as queso Oaxaca—is sold rolled up like balls of yarn in various sizes. It is similar to mozzarella in flavor and behaves not unlike the string cheese sticks you might have eaten as a kid: To use it, you have to unravel the cheese and pull it apart into threads. Quesillo is often stuffed into quesadillas or used to top *tlayudas,* a common antojito in Oaxaca. It's also pretty tasty browned directly in a pan, doused with salsa, and eaten straight with a fork and knife.

MOLCAJETE

This traditional Mexican kitchen tool is a shallow, three-legged mortar carved from volcanic rock, with a matching tejolote (pestle). Used to grind spices and compound salsas, a molcajete gives you a level of textural control that can't be achieved using a blender—molcajetes crush the food rather than mincing or processing it. Molcajetes are easy to find at kitchen supply stores; they season themselves over time, and because they are made of porous rock that absorbs aromas, they gain character with use, like a cast-iron skillet. To maintain that patina, don't run the molcajete through the dishwasher or use any harsh detergents. Simply rinse with water and dry with a cloth towel.

THE CHILES IN THIS BOOK

Chile varieties represent an infinite universe—a book unto themselves and a subject far too vast to cover with comprehensive authority in these pages. The vernacular itself can be a moving target: the same kind of chile may go by one name when it is fresh and another when it's dried, and there are regional colloquialisms to parse, too. For this book, I selected chiles that can realistically be purchased in the United States, and I stuck with the nomenclature you're most likely to encounter at the grocery store.

ANCHO

Dark brown and triangular in shape, ancho chiles are actually just dried, fully ripe poblano chiles. They taste tangy, like dried fruit with a slight green note, and while they are generally not that spicy, you'll occasionally find an angry one in the litter. Along with guajillos, anchos are one of the workhorse chiles of the Mexican kitchen: abundant, inexpensive, and ubiquitous in many traditional recipes.

ÁRBOL

Small—about 2 or 3 inches long—smooth-skinned and slender, chiles de árbol are often used in thin "hot sauce"-style salsas, or are toasted until crisp and ground into powder. They have the bright, vegetal flavor of a bell pepper with none of the sweetness, and they're hot as hell. It takes some finesse to tame the burn of these things and perceive their other flavors: seeding, toasting, and soaking the chiles helps, but they'll never be anything close to mild, no matter what you do. Árbols are always sold dried; I've never seen them fresh in the United States. When you're shopping, you want to see bright red skin; if they have become brownish, they are showing their age. Also, be careful not to confuse árbols with Thai bird's-eye chiles, which look similar but have a totally different profile.

CHIPOTLE

Many dried chiles are just left out in the sun to dehydrate, but because jalapeños have such a high water content, they'll rot under those conditions. Instead, jalapeños are smoke-dried, a process that yields the delicious chipotle. There are two types of chipotle chiles. The large ones are known as chipotles mecos—they develop a cork-colored patina when fully ripe and turn sandy-brown when dried. The more common chipotle mora or morita is smaller (1½-3 inches) and takes on a deep red, almost black hue when dried. Both are quite spicy; to me, the mecos taste grassier while the moras have a deeper molasses flavor. Use whichever you can get your hands on. Chipotles are also often sold canned in a thick tomato sauce with garlic and spices. These are delicious and incredibly convenient to work with because they're already hydrated, but keep in mind that the sauce will introduce its own flavor.

GUAJILLO

Like anchos, dried, bright-red guajillos are one of the most common chiles in Mexican cooking. The guajillos I've encountered in Mexico seem to be a bit spicier than the ones I've tasted in America, but generally they have a berry-like flavor with very faint sweetness. Because of their mild heat and large size (4-6 inches), guajillos are often used to bulk up the base of a salsa and carry the flavor of other, more assertive chiles. Guajillo-based salsas are great for things like enchiladas and chilaquiles.

CHILE SEEDS AND VEINS

Capsaicin is the naturally occurring chemical that makes chile peppers hot. Most of it is concentrated in the pepper's membranes and placenta (the central vein, where the seeds attach). Removing the seeds and veins will significantly temper the heat of certain chiles, like jalapeños, but I find that the effect is less apparent with hotter chiles—habaneros and serranos are going to be pretty spicy even if you scrape them. For purposes of this book, I indicated seeding and veining the chiles where I thought it made sense to do so, but it's a personal preference. If you want to add more heat, leave the seeds and veins intact; if you prefer a more mild burn, remove and discard them.

HABANERO

These plump, roundish little chiles are some of the hottest in the world, but they also offer notes of tropical fruit and herbs—a unique flavor profile you won't find in other varieties. Most habaneros start out light green and later ripen to yellow and then to deep orange. There are some rarer varieties that ripen to dark purple or even chocolate brown, but the flavor is not markedly different. Habaneros are very common in the Yucatán, where they frequently season table salsas. When shopping in the United States, be careful not to mistake Scotch bonnet chiles for habaneros—they look very similar.

JALAPEÑO

The most commonly known chile outside of Mexico, spicy jalapeños are typically about 2 or 3 inches in length and have a bright green, grassy flavor. They are named after Xalapa Veracruz, the region of Mexico where they were originally cultivated. When jalapeños are smoke-dried, they are known as chipotles, but they are also delicious raw, roasted, or pickled. Try charring them and stuffing them with cheese, breading them, and then deep-frying them. I invented this. I call it a jalapeño popper.

PASILLA

The word pasilla is used to indicate a dried chilaca chile. They are typically 5 or 6 inches long with a chocolaty color and moderate heat (but you'll occasionally encounter one that is ripping hot). Their rich and meaty profile makes them pair well with red meat, game, and mushrooms. Note that in Oaxaca this chile is called pasilla Mexicana to distinguish it from the local pasilla Oaxaqueño.

HANDLING CHILES

When handling fresh or dried chiles, keep in mind that capsaicin has some serious hang time on the skin and it isn't water soluble—that means that even after washing your hands, you will need to be careful about touching sensitive areas on your body, especially your eyes. Wear rubber gloves if you want to play it safe. When shopping for dried chiles, look for a supple, leathery texture that's neither brittle nor damp. Also, remember that just because something is dried, that does not mean it lasts forever: Store dried chiles in an airtight container and toss them if they begin to feel too fragile.

PASILLA OAXAQUEÑO

This is my favorite chile, and if I had my way, I'd put them in everything. Pasillas Oaxaqueños taste like spicy smoked raspberries, are dark in color with deep-red tones, and their size varies anywhere from 1 to 4 inches. They aren't cheap, but are worth a splurge. Buy them from spice houses like Terra Spice or from specialty produce purveyors such as Fresh and Wild. If you come across a chile relleno in Oaxaca, it's likely made with the largest specimen of this chile: stuffed with picadillo, fried, and placed on a tortilla.

PIQUÍN

I use this chile exclusively in its powdered form in this book, but super-spicy piquíns also make their way into hot sauces (there's some in Cholula). At about ¼ inch, piquíns are too small to seed—the name means "small chile" and is used in Mexico to refer to many varieties of tiny dried chiles. I have seen them fresh in Mexico, but they are almost exclusively sold dried in the United States. Find them in little packets in the dried chile section of your grocery store.

POBLANO

These fresh, triangular chiles are large—4 to 6 inches in length—with a deep green hue and varying heat level. Poblanos are ideal for chiles rellenos because of their size and thick flesh. When roasted, peeled, and cut into strips, they are called rajas. If poblanos are allowed to ripen and then dry in the sun, they are known as anchos.

SERRANO

These small green chiles are used both raw and roasted for a wide range of Mexican salsas, especially salsa verde. They look like miniature jalapeños, but are significantly spicier, and the seeds and veins are not typically removed. You can substitute jalapeños if you can't find serranos or if you simply want to turn down the Scoville rating of your salsa.

TORTILLAS

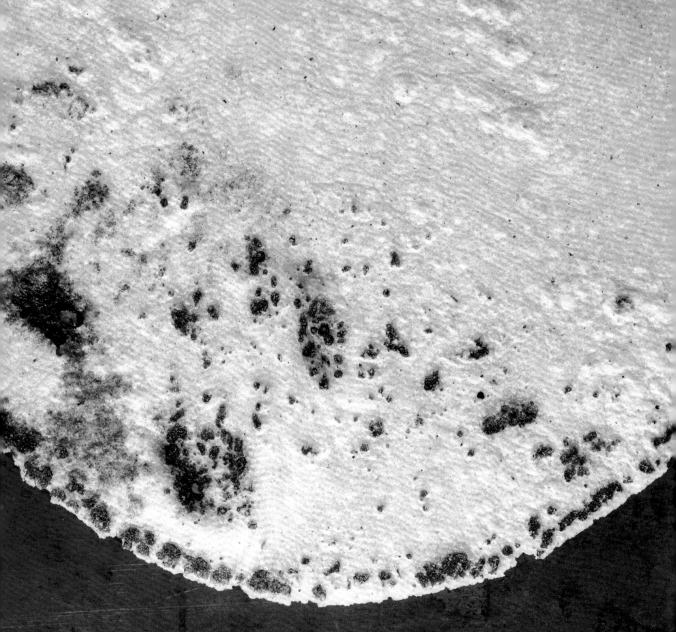

This book is as much a discussion of preparing tacos as it is a record of the twisty road I took to understand them. That journey starts with the foundation of a good taco:

THE TORTILLA

When I build a taco, I often think about sushi. A piece of mackerel or geoduck clam may be beautiful on its own, but it takes on new dimension draped over a mound of perfect vinegared rice. I feel the same way about the influence of a fresh tortilla. Just like sushi rice, a tortilla is so much more than its function of delivering food to mouth. It can offer some of the most stirring and intangible flavors in the culinary universe and is the single make-or-break factor that separates a forgettable taco from an epiphany. A tortilla is not a background player. It isn't goddamn Muzak. A fresh tortilla is the kind of thing you notice, and once you taste a good one, you won't be able to tolerate anything else.

My stance here is firm: There is absolutely no substitute for a fresh, home-made tortilla, and suggesting any kind of store-bought alternative would keep me up at night. To fully use this book as it's intended, you have to reconcile to the idea of making your own. Consider the pages that follow an argument for why that's worth doing, and, of course, how to go about doing it.

This section begins with some background on corn, and what it means to take the grain from kernel to masa to tortilla. From there, it looks at the world of wheat flour, and then explores some ideas for manipulating both masa and wheat doughs with nontraditional ingredients.

Corn and flour tortillas each have their own virtues, and for the most part we've avoided making specific suggestions as to which type best suits each taco in this book. Experiment with both, or play with some of the flavored riffs explored later in this chapter. Ultimately, the choice of canvas boils down to personal taste; cook what works for you.

What you need to know about corn

BEFORE WE CAN TALK ABOUT MASA, WE NEED TO TALK ABOUT CORN.

The vast majority of corn grown on this planet isn't the sweet summer stalk you know—most of it is field corn and it wouldn't be welcome at any cookout. Sweet corn is essentially a novelty crop in most parts of the world (think of the way you perceive blood oranges as more exotic than basic navel oranges, and you'll get the idea). But it is the dense, starchy, low-sugar field corn that keeps the earth spinning. It's the basis for almost every crinkly bag of chips in the junk food aisle, as well as the high-fructose syrup that sweetens our soda pop and Skittles. It is in our pig and cattle feed. It is refined into oils and starches that make up everything from adhesives and ethanol to toothpaste and cosmetics. Field corn, essentially, rules the world.

It also fills a gap in understanding we have in this country in terms of the way we think about corn. It's fair to say that Americans largely treat sweet corn as a vegetable—we slather it with butter and eat it off the cob on the Fourth of July, or we throw it in with shellfish for Chesapeake and Lowcountry boils. But corn is not a vegetable, it's a grain. The applications of field corn, especially in a Mexican culinary context, help drive that lesson home: Just as wheat or rye would be processed into dough for our bread, field corn can become masa—the fat-free, gluten-free wonder dough used throughout Latin America to shape tamales, pound out pupusas and arepas, and, of course, form tortillas.

But that takes some work. Field corn kernels are encased in a thick hull called a pericarp that is difficult to digest. To dissolve that hull and transform the corn into something edible, it first needs to be treated with an alkaline solution of water and calcium oxide—a mineral sold as "cal" in Mexico or "pickling lime" in the United States. That process is called nixtamalization.

What Is Nixtamalization?

Nixtamalization may be the best example of the ancient and impeccable logic embedded in the Mexican diet. The Aztecs and Mayans learned that if they boiled their corn with limestone or ash from the cooking fire, it changed its qualities for the better. It softened the kernel and enhanced its aroma and flavor. They might have also noticed over time that the process improved their health—nixtamalization makes vitamins like niacin already present in the corn available for absorption by the body. In fact, cultures that base their diets on corn without adopting nixtamalization have historically been plagued with vitamin deficiency diseases, like pellagra.

Nixtamalization was early, intuitive science. But thousands of years later we're still doing it in much the same way, for exactly the same reasons: nixtamalized corn tastes better, smells better, and is healthier and easier to eat.

Making Nixtamal

Grind nixtamal and you get masa, the foundational foodstuff of Mexico. Making nixtamal is an education unto itself, and it's worth doing for the same reasons that baking bread from scratch is important: it connects you with the ancients and instills an appreciation for the simple, nethermost foods we take for granted. I've found that without a major investment in specialized equipment, it's almost impossible to grind masa finely enough for tortillas at home. Although homemade nixtamal is too coarse for tortillas, it's great for pozole and for things like sopes, huaraches, and other antojitos made with masa.

The first challenge in making nixtamal is finding dried, whole-kernel corn, which is more difficult than it sounds. I like the white and yellow varieties sold by Honeyville and Rovey Seed Co. But these companies sell in 50-pound increments, so when you're done experimenting with nixtamal, you'll have an unmanageable amount of leftover grain.

If you don't want to use the excess to stock the pantry in your weird neighbor's doomsday shelter, you can buy from Masienda, a New York–based company that imports diverse landrace corn from small Mexican farms. You can request a catalog of their regional varieties and order sample sizes (about 5 pounds) via masienda.com. You'll also need food-grade pickling lime or cal, which is fairly easy to track down. The heirloom grain company Anson Mills sells it, and it's readily available online.

There is no standard when it comes to preparing nixtamal, and the ideal timing, temperature, and ratio will vary wildly depending on the kind of corn you use. There are innumerable varieties grown in Mexico, each with its own distinctive terroir. But more importantly—for the purposes of making nixtamal, anyway—these different strains fluctuate in their starch, sugar, and moisture contents, all of which modify the cooking time.

To further complicate things, just like with bread baking, there are external elements such as humidity and elevation that can affect the outcome.

NIXTAMAL

We designed this formula to produce 1 pound of masa, which is our standard measurement in the corn tortilla recipes. Working with such a small volume has an appreciable effect on the cooking time—the water loses its residual heat much more quickly than it would with a larger batch, so you have to boil the corn for longer. What you're looking for in the finished kernel is a 50:50 ratio of cooked exterior to raw, chalky core. You'll need to play around with the various components to develop your own recipe and get this right, but here's a good place to start:

NIXTAMAL
MAKES 1 POUND

½ pound dried whole-kernel field corn

1 ounce pickling lime (cal),* dissolved in ½ cup water

*Do not taste the pickling lime (cal) on its own—it will burn your tongue. Also, wash your hands after working with it to avoid getting any in your eyes.

Place the corn kernels in a 2-quart saucepan and add enough water to cover by 1 inch (about 3 cups). Bring to a boil over high heat and let it boil for 10 minutes. Remove the pot from the heat, mix in the lime solution with a wooden spoon and let sit at room temperature for at least 12 hours.

Drain the soaked corn in a large colander and massage the kernels under running water. You will notice your hands begin to feel slimy as the friction causes the softened hulls to dissolve and rinse away. As you are massaging the corn, keep an eye out for stray stones to pick out and discard, as you would for dried beans. When the kernels look clean, you're done. Taste the corn; it should be slightly softened but still quite raw inside, and it should taste—like corn, obviously. This is nixtamal.

Grinding the Masa

You know those movies that begin by telling you that the narrator will be dead by the end of it, and the whole thing is just designed to make you fall in love with this omnipotent voice and then wrench it from you before the credits roll? That's what this section is. Sorry in advance for breaking your heart.

The thing is, grinding nixtamal into masa that is fine enough to use for tortillas isn't easy. To do it at Empellón, we use a high-voltage, five-horsepower, 1,200-pound hunk of metal fitted with hand-chiseled volcanic stones. It can grind about 50 pounds of masa in 5 minutes. You probably don't have one of these lying around.

For this book, I decided to look into a few common kitchen appliances to see if they could get the job done. A stand mixer fitted with a meat grinder attachment wasn't up to the task—the nixtamal couldn't pass through the finest die without clogging it, and the larger die produced a dough that was too coarse and pebbly. Next, I tried a food processor, adding water to the nixtamal to help it pass through the blades. The finished masa was smooth, but too wet and sticky to work with. I tried multi-step methods, combining the stand mixer and the food processor, and even incorporating a sifting step to try to refine the dough. I wasn't satisfied with any of the results.

Of course, masa predates the industrial revolution by a few thousand years, so you might be wondering if there's an ancient solution to this problem. There is, but you might not like it. Mesoamericans were of tougher stock than we are today, and they ground their masa by hand using stone tools called metates and manos. Grains were crushed and ground as the heavy mano—a rolling-pin–like pestle—scraped against the surface of the metate slab. You can still buy these today, but it is tedious work for the modern cook. If you've got the will, though, have at it.

If you want to preserve the poetry of hand-ground masa, you could experiment with a manual molino de maiz—a top-loading corn mill equipped with stone or cast-iron grinding plates and a table-mount clamp. I experimented with a few of these and had success in grinding nixtamal into masa, but the resulting dough still wasn't fine enough for tortillas, even when I passed it through the grinder twice. You could use this masa for tamales or sopes, though, and be perfectly happy with it.

So now you know why I warned you. I've yet to find a reliable method using common kitchen equipment to grind masa that's fine enough for tortillas. And frankly, that's okay. Until I purchased an industrial corn grinder for Empellón, we didn't make our own masa, either. We bought it from a tortilla factory, and if you live in a city with a Mexican population, you can probably do the same. Buy masa on the day you plan to make tortillas and store it at room temperature—refrigeration will dry out the dough.

And if you can't buy fresh masa, there's still hope. For you, there's masa harina.

In Defense of Masa Harina

I'll say right up front that masa harina is an imperfect solution. The same way there's no comparing Folger's to coffee made with freshly ground beans, it's hard to measure masa harina—an instant flour made from dehydrated masa—against fresh masa dough. There's just a certain vitality lost in the drying process.

Still, masa harina is readily available in most well-stocked grocery stores, and with the addition of a little water, it approximates the texture and flavor of the fresh dough. A warm tortilla prepared with harina may not hit the same celestial notes as one made with fresh masa, but it is still an absolute revelation if all you've ever tasted is reheated, store-bought tortillas. There's irrefutable value in that, so I stand by it.

For our Corn Tortilla recipe (page 35), I provide measurements for both fresh masa and masa harina. But once the flour has been hydrated, you can use masa harina in any recipe that calls for fresh masa in identical proportions. In some cases where masa is called for as a thickener—such as for the Mole Verde (page 86) or the green chorizo gravy in the Sunnyside Duck Egg Tacos (page 217)—you don't even need to hydrate it before incorporating. When you're shopping for masa harina, note that you'll sometimes hear it referred to as "Maseca," which is one of the most prevalent brands. Bob's Red Mill also makes a good version.

CORN TORTILLAS

It's hard to call something with only one ingredient a recipe. Making tortillas is really just a method, and getting it right depends on a lot of little details. Make enough tortillas, and you'll learn to intuit when your dough is too dry or too sticky, as well as how to correct it. You'll acclimate to the tortilla press, figuring out exactly how much pressure you need to apply to yield a perfect, uniformly thick round every time. You'll develop muscle memory as you slide tortillas onto the hot griddle, and agility as you pull them off the heat the moment they begin to blister. It requires some finesse, but making tortillas is a critical threshold in grasping Mexican cuisine, and it is the baseline skill you'll need to get the most out of this book.

I've designed this recipe to make 12 tortillas to match my taco yields. But I've found that fresh tortillas rarely go uneaten, so I often double the recipe. Consider doing the same, especially for your first few attempts. There's a "first pancake" effect at play when you're making tortillas, and you may need to toss a few failures until you get the hang of it.

Time is also vital to keep in mind, since masa tortillas are at their best when they are still hot from the griddle—see page 38 for suggestions on how to hold them at temperature.

MAKES 12 TORTILLAS

---

1 pound fresh masa, or 1½ cups
    masa harina kneaded with
    1 cup water

EQUIPMENT: Tortilla press*

*I use a 7½-inch cast-iron press, which should be easy to find for less than $20. Note that cast-iron can rust if not properly cared for; keep it dry, and lightly rub it with oil if you are storing the press for a long time without regular use.

INSPECT THE DOUGH: Whether you're using fresh masa or rehydrated masa harina, you want the texture to be as soft and moist as possible without sticking to your hands. If the dough develops small cracks when squeezed, it is too dry and needs more moisture. To correct this, knead water into the dough in 1 tablespoon increments until it becomes malleable and forms into a ball. Cover the masa with a damp towel.

PREPARE THE EQUIPMENT: Set up a double griddle or two cast-iron pans over two burners. Heat one side of the griddle (or one pan) over low-medium heat and the other over medium-high heat for about 5 minutes.

Cut two squares of medium-heavy plastic to fit the press (a freezer bag works nicely). Open the tortilla press and place one square on the bottom plate and the other on the top plate, making sure the plastic does not wrinkle.

MAKE A TEST TORTILLA: Grab a small handful of the masa and roll it into a sphere about the size of a golf ball. Gently flatten it into a rough disk with your fingers.

Position the tortilla press with the pressure handle on the side of your body that you favor—if you're right-handed, the handle should be on the right. Open the press, keeping the plastic squares on each plate. Center the disk of masa

recipe continues

on the bottom plate. Close the top plate, ensuring that the second piece of plastic lands squarely on top of the dough. Fold the handle and apply even pressure. Fold back the handle and open the press. Peel the top plastic from the tortilla. The tortilla should be 5½ inches in diameter and about ⅛ inch thick.

Pick up the bottom plastic square with the tortilla stuck to it. If you're right-handed, pick it up with your left hand; if you're left-handed, pick it up with your right. Flip the tortilla over onto your empty palm; the upper edge should run along the tops of your index and middle fingers. Peel off the plastic.

COOK THE TORTILLA: Position yourself over the cooler end of the griddle, with the tortilla draped over your palm and the top of your hand parallel to the hot surface. Bring the edge of the tortilla to the griddle and very quickly slide your hand out from under it; the tortilla should stick right away to the surface. If you're too slow, the tortilla will fold and cook unevenly.

Cook for 15 seconds. The tortilla will begin to change color after 10 seconds. Using a metal spatula or your fingers, flip it onto the hotter side of the griddle and cook for 30 seconds. Flip the tortilla again, leaving it on the hotter side and cook for another 10 seconds before flipping a final time. Cook for an additional 10 seconds. When the tortilla is done, its edges will begin to release from the griddle and it may inflate slightly.

TASTE YOUR TEST TORTILLA: If the dough is too dry, the texture will be heavy and the edges will begin to crack. If needed, gradually add water to the remaining dough in 1 teaspoon increments until it is moist and malleable.

Once you're happy with the texture, divide the remaining dough into 12 equal balls and repeat the process of pressing and griddling the tortillas. Store the cooked tortillas in an insulated container so that they retain their heat until ready to serve (see page 38).

A NOTE ON STORING TORTILLAS

If my refrain about the importance of warm tortillas hasn't yet seared itself into your frontal lobe, here it is again: The difference between a great taco and a crappy taco is in the tortilla. It's that vital.

Even more specifically, the difference lies in a tortilla that retains some of the initial heat used to cook it, especially when you're working with masa. Reheated tortillas are brittle because the starch doesn't react well when it is cooled and warmed up again. There's a lot of long-winded science to support this, but basically it's that the starch in masa tortillas is malleable when warm, but cools into a non-thermoreversible gel—a gel that cannot return to a fluid state once it is completely cooled.

You could metabolize all of that information, or you could just think of it this way: If you've ever had a taco fall apart on you while you were eating it, then you know what can happen when a tortilla is cooled and then rewarmed. It loses its elasticity and can disintegrate.

So now you know: Once you've cooked tortillas, you have to keep them warm until you're ready to serve them.

We decided to run some tests to find out which storage options perform the best over a longer period. We selected seven vessels designed for insulation. We tested each container separately, filling each with an identical stack of 12 just-made masa tortillas. Once the tortillas were positioned inside each vessel, we placed a thermocouple probe between tortillas 6 and 7, closed the lid, and measured the initial temperature—usually between 180 and 190° Fahrenheit. We then documented the temperature every 30 minutes for 2 hours while keeping the vessels closed and undisturbed in a room-temperature environment.

We were looking for sustained warmth, but we were also watching for other degradation factors, such as dryness or, in some cases, the effect of condensation. (No one wants a soggy tortilla.) We determined that 120°F is the threshold for tortillas that are suitable for immediate use. We also found that tortillas that had dropped below that threshold could be revived with a brief reheat in a cast-iron pan—if they retain even a bit of their initial heat, the starch is still fluid enough to bounce back.

Of the seven test vessels, the top performer was the most surprising: a thick fabric tortilla warmer covered with culturally insensitive dancing chiles that we found on Amazon for $8. After a 2-hour lapse, the tortillas were still supple and ready to eat, and the oven mitt material had wicked away any condensation. We were also impressed with the results of our MacGyver rig: We wrapped a heating pad in plastic wrap and folded it around the tortillas. After 2 hours, the tortillas had lost only about a quarter of their heat and were ready for serving. If you go this route, be careful not to buy a heating pad with an automatic turn-off feature.

The rest of the storage options dropped below the 120°F threshold after 1 hour. Of these, a small insulated beach cooler and a standard-issue fiberglass tortilla holder had the highest finishing temperatures, so they are the best bets if you need to store tortillas for a full 2 hours and are willing to reheat them. We tested a Styrofoam holder and found it created a lot of condensation, while a woven plastic basket left the tortillas dry. Both of these vessels rapidly lost their heat after just 30 minutes. A cast-iron Dutch oven with the lid wrapped in a moist towel was also unsuccessful at room temperature, but it worked beautifully when held in a low-heat oven. Note that this is a better option only when you're working with a large batch of tortillas; after an hour the steam from the moist towel begins to break down the top and bottom tortillas in the stack, and that's a meaningful loss when you have only 12 to begin with.

So what's the best move here? Well, if you need to hold your tortillas warm only for 30 minutes, just about any storage solution will work, so take your pick. But if you want to push it a little longer and avoid the hassle of reheating, I say spring for a fabric pouch—racist imagery optional—and call it a day.

FLOUR TORTILLAS

There's a tacit understanding in much of Mexico that the word tortilla implies a product made with corn. In the United States, I'd say the opposite is true. It's telling that the term gringa is sometimes used in Mexico to indicate a flour tortilla, and that many of the fast-Mex chains on this side of the border don't even list soft corn tortillas on their menus—just crispy corn shells or wheat flour wraps. In fact, flour tortillas are so naturalized into the American diet that it's easy to forget they do have a traditional foothold in Mexico, particularly in the arid northern regions where wheat grows more easily than corn.

Flour tortillas actually powered Empellón for our first few years. When Taqueria opened, we were going through more than 2,000 hand-pressed corn tortillas a week—so much volume that my cooks were developing repetitive stress injuries. We simply couldn't match production to demand while keeping the quality where we wanted it.

It was a conversation with a food writer friend that got me thinking. He told me that the flour tortillas he ate in Mexico were the best tortillas of any kind he'd ever tasted. When he came in for dinner, my wife, Lauren, prepared a batch of forty as a tribute. We sent six of them to the writer's table with some queso fundido; in seconds, my kitchen staff had demolished the rest.

That was a teachable moment. At the time I had this idea that flour tortillas weren't equal to the mission of my restaurant—that it would be dishonorable in some way to serve them. I cringe to think of how shortsighted that was. Of course, there are good versions and bad versions of everything we enjoy eating. There are supermarket flour tortillas that are mealy and packed with enough preservatives to keep them shelf-immortal. And there are the good ones: elastic and almost biscuit-like, enriched with lard, hand-stretched, and freckled with char on a hot griddle.

I discovered that, in addition to being delicious, flour tortillas are also more forgiving than corn tortillas: they hold their texture for longer and can withstand reheating. Their resilience made such a difference in our ability to keep pace in the kitchen that we switched exclusively to flour until we could invest in the corn tortilla machine that now supplies all of our restaurants. Even then, we couldn't kick our love for flour, and to this day we serve both.

The method for preparing flour tortillas is very similar to that of corn, with a few small distinctions. Because this dough contains gluten, you need to be careful not to overwork it as you mix and knead, or the finished tortillas will be tough. To form the rounds, you should use a rolling pin rather than a tortilla press to get the dough properly thin.

recipe continues

And while flour tortillas, like corn, are at their very best hot off the griddle, they won't die if you reheat them. Cool the tortillas, stack them, and wrap in plastic. Hold at room temperature until you're ready to warm them using a cast-iron skillet.

Note that the flaky texture and slight richness that make flour tortillas so compelling are derived from lard. I've found that vegetable shortening is a poor substitute here, so if you're cooking for vegetarians, corn is the way to go.

MAKES 12 TORTILLAS

---

4 cups all-purpose flour, plus more as needed

½ cup lard

1 teaspoon kosher salt

MAKE THE DOUGH: In a stand mixer fitted with the paddle attachment, combine the flour, lard, and salt and mix on low speed until mealy, about 2 minutes. Add 1 cup of water and continue mixing until the dough just comes together, about another minute.

Transfer the dough to a smooth work surface and knead gently, being careful to not overwork it—you want the dough smooth and elastic. Cover the dough with a damp towel and let rest for 10 minutes.

PREPARE THE EQUIPMENT: Set up a double griddle or 2 cast-iron pans over two burners. Heat one side of the griddle (or one pan) over low-medium heat and the other over medium-high heat for about 5 minutes.

MAKE A TEST TORTILLA: Grab a handful of the dough and roll it into a sphere about the size of a golf ball, setting the rest aside beneath the towel.

Using a rolling pin, roll out the ball of dough into a 6-inch round. You may need to flour the surface to keep the tortilla from sticking. (If the tortilla is too sticky, the dough is too wet; knead in some additional flour, a little at a time, until the dough is workable.)

COOK THE TORTILLA: Position yourself over the cooler end of the griddle, with the tortilla draped over your palm and the top of your hand parallel to the hot surface. Bring the edge of the tortilla to the griddle and very quickly slide your hand out from under it; the tortilla should stick right away to the surface. If you're too slow, the tortilla will fold and cook unevenly.

Cook for 15 seconds. The tortilla will slightly change color after 10 seconds. Using a metal spatula or your fingers, flip it onto the hotter side of the griddle and cook for 30 seconds. Flip it once again, leaving it on the hotter side and cook for another 10 seconds before flipping a final time. Cook for an additional 10 seconds. When the tortilla is done, its edges will begin to release from the griddle and it may inflate slightly.

TASTE YOUR TEST TORTILLA: If the dough is too dry, the texture will be heavy and the edges will begin to crack. If needed, gradually add water to the dough in 1 teaspoon increments until it is moist and malleable.

Once you're happy with the texture, divide the remaining dough into 12 equal balls and repeat the process of rolling out the tortillas and griddling them one by one. Store the cooked tortillas in an insulated container so that they retain their heat until ready to serve (see page 38).

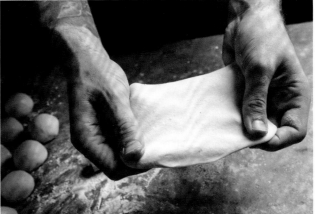

NEO-TRADITIONAL TORTILLAS

Because I came out of the wd~50 kitchen—where peanut butter could find its way into pasta noodles and a falafel ball might conceal a core of liquid foie gras—there's an expectation that I'm a chef who can't help but tinker with food. And to a certain extent that's correct. Working with Wylie Dufresne at wd~50 and Grant Achatz at Alinea taught me to consider how food is framed, and helped me think outside of ingrained techniques and flavor pairings. Those are lessons that will always inform the work that I do.

But I didn't always want to be innovative back then. Sometimes I just wanted to make a really tasty vanilla ice cream. As I settled into Empellón, I began to value the satisfaction that comes with simply discovering an old recipe and preparing it well. Creative freedom takes many forms, and as a chef I want the flexibility to explore both ends of the spectrum: cooking in deference to the classics or in defiance of them. So while this book exalts the traditions of corn and flour tortillas, I like to think it also presents the taco as an idea worthy of creative scrutiny. To that end, this section contemplates the tortilla and explores some of the possibilities that open up when the basic recipe is manipulated.

Tortillas are a great canvas after all, and they take exceptionally well to elaboration. What happens when you build tortillas using alternative starches and grains? Enhance them with vegetable juices? Or enrich them with animal proteins like pork or poultry? The recipes that follow are designed to crack open your creative window. This section grew out of questions we asked ourselves; as you read through it, I hope you'll ask some of your own.

ALTERNATIVE MASA HARINA TORTILLAS

I've talked about the limitations of masa harina, but working with a dried product can also provide a creative advantage. Instead of reconstituting the harina with water, we experimented with vegetable juices and spice infusions to embed flavor in the tortilla itself. Here are a few of our favorite discoveries.

BEET TORTILLAS

Fresh beet juice imparts a vegetal flavor and dyes these tortillas a show-stopping fuchsia. They work well with anything that can match the root's earthiness: Huitlacoche Tacos (page 202) or Mixed Mushroom Tacos (page 208), or just a smear of tangy goat cheese and crumbled walnuts.

Because beets have such a high sugar content, tortillas hydrated with pure beet juice have a tendency to caramelize and stiffen on the griddle before they are cooked through. Diluting the juice with a bit of water as you knead the dough helps the tortillas stay soft and supple. Keep that in mind if you want to experiment with other sugary vegetables, like carrots.

MAKES 12 TORTILLAS

6 medium beets, peeled and diced

1½ cups masa harina

Run the diced beets through a juicer. Set up a fine-mesh sieve over a bowl and pass the juice through the strainer.

In a large bowl, combine the masa harina with 1 cup of the beet juice and ¼ cup of water. Knead the mixture gently until it is as soft and moist as possible without sticking to your hands.

INSPECT THE DOUGH: If the dough develops small cracks when squeezed, it is too dry and needs more moisture. To correct this, knead water into the dough in 1 tablespoon increments until it becomes malleable and forms into a ball. Cover the dough with a damp towel.

Follow the instructions on pages 35–36 to press and cook the tortillas.

SAFFRON TORTILLAS

It turns out that tortillas are a particularly lovely application for one of the world's most rarified ingredients. A steeped saffron tea added to masa harina yields a psychedelic-looking dough, marbled in orange swirls that stretch and warp as you knead. The saffron infuses a soft bitterness and a perfume that make me think of Spanish paella. I serve these with any seafood taco, or even with the Raw Porcini Mushrooms with Savory Arroz con Leche (page 206).

MAKES 12 TORTILLAS

½ gram (about ¼ teaspoon) saffron threads

1½ cups masa harina

In a small bowl, combine the saffron with 1 cup of warm water and let steep for 5 minutes.

Place the masa harina in a large bowl. Pour in the saffron infusion and knead the mixture gently until the saffron is evenly distributed throughout and the dough is as soft and moist as possible without sticking to your hands.

INSPECT THE DOUGH: If the dough develops small cracks when squeezed, it is too dry and needs more moisture. To correct this, knead water into the dough in 1 tablespoon increments until it becomes malleable and forms into a ball. Cover the dough with a damp towel.

Follow the instructions on pages 35–36 to press and cook the tortillas.

TORTILLAS WITH INCLUSIONS

In pastry vernacular, an "inclusion" is something that adds texture and flavor to ice creams and cakes—things like chocolate chips or crushed nuts. The idea maps beautifully onto tortilla making. You can incorporate greens, nuts, spices, or herbs while kneading your masa to transform its flavor and consistency. When working with inclusions, make sure that whatever you are adding to the dough is finely and evenly chopped. Large or jagged pieces will cause the tortilla to crumble.

PISTACHIO TORTILLAS

Pistachios contribute more than distinctive flavor when added to masa. Unlike flour tortillas, masa doesn't contain fat, so the oily nuts have an enriching effect that's uncommon for this kind of dough. Sautéed vegetables with nuts is a classic pairing, so stuff these tortillas with any kind of wilted greens. Wild Spinach Tacos (page 211) would be perfect.

MAKES 12 TORTILLAS

1 pound fresh masa, or 1½ cups masa harina kneaded with 1 cup water

1 cup raw, unsalted pistachios, shelled and finely chopped

Place the masa and chopped pistachios in a large bowl and knead gently until the nuts are evenly distributed throughout.

INSPECT THE DOUGH: You want the texture to be as soft and moist as possible without sticking to your hands. If the dough develops small cracks when squeezed, it is too dry and needs more moisture. To correct this, knead water into the dough in 1 tablespoon increments until it becomes malleable and forms into a ball. Cover the dough with a damp towel.

Follow the instructions on pages 35–36 to press and cook the tortillas.

SPINACH TORTILLAS

Eat these wholesome tortillas with a piece of steamed or grilled fish, or just a pat of butter, a pinch of nutmeg, and salt. When incorporating blanched greens into masa, remember that certain varieties—especially spinach—hang on to moisture like a sponge. You really need to work to squeeze out the water or the dough will be too sticky.

MAKES 12 TORTILLAS

1 pound fresh masa, or 1½ cups masa harina kneaded with 1 cup water

¼ pound spinach leaves, blanched, squeezed very dry, and finely chopped

Place the masa and chopped spinach in a large bowl and knead gently until the greens are evenly distributed throughout.

INSPECT THE DOUGH: You want the texture to be as soft and moist as possible without sticking to your hands. If the dough develops small cracks when squeezed, it is too dry and needs more moisture. To correct this, knead water into the dough in 1 tablespoon increments until it becomes malleable and forms into a ball. Cover the dough with a damp towel.

Follow the instructions on pages 35–36 to press and cook the tortillas.

TORTILLAS MADE FROM ALTERNATIVE GRAINS

Masa is the basis for most of these neo-traditional recipes, but the ones that follow are variations on flour. Switching up the grain yields tortillas that nod to other international carb customs, like French crêpes or Scandinavian rye bread sandwiches.

BUCKWHEAT TORTILLAS

The flavor of these tortillas reminds me of the Breton tradition of savory buckwheat galettes. Just like the French pancakes, these are great stuffed with eggs, cheese, charcuterie, or fish, such as the Smoked Salmon Tacos with Salmon Roe Salsa (page 185).

MAKES 12 TORTILLAS

3 cups all-purpose flour

1 cup buckwheat flour

½ cup lard

1 teaspoon kosher salt

In a stand mixer fitted with the paddle attachment, combine the all-purpose and buckwheat flours, lard, and salt and mix on low speed until mealy, about 2 minutes. Add 1 cup of water and continue mixing until the dough just comes together, about another minute.

Transfer the dough to a smooth work surface and knead gently, being careful to not overwork it.

INSPECT THE DOUGH: You want it to be smooth and elastic. Cover the dough with a damp towel and let rest for 10 minutes.

Follow the instructions on pages 42–43 to roll out and cook the tortillas.

RYE TORTILLAS

Rye flour gives these tortillas a malty richness. They are a natural match for Pastrami Tacos (page 123), or you could give a nod to Scandinavian smørbrød—open-faced rye bread sandwiches—and serve these with smoked or pickled fish.

MAKES 12 TORTILLAS

3 cups all-purpose flour

1 cup rye flour

½ cup lard

1 teaspoon kosher salt

In a stand mixer fitted with the paddle attachment, combine the all-purpose and rye flours, lard, and salt and mix on low speed until mealy, about 2 minutes. Add 1 cup of water and continue mixing until the dough just comes together, about another minute.

Transfer the dough to a smooth work surface and knead gently, being careful to not overwork it.

INSPECT THE DOUGH: You want it to be smooth and elastic. Cover the dough with a damp towel and let rest for 10 minutes.

Follow the instructions on pages 42–43 to roll out and cook the tortillas.

TORTILLAS STRETCHED WITH STARCHY VEGETABLES

In her book *Oaxaca al Gusto*, Diana Kennedy describes encountering masa tortillas boosted with starchy vegetables like yuca and plantain—a fix devised to help stretch the corn during scarce seasons. The tortillas in this section run with that idea. You can also try experimenting with things like winter squash, turnips, or parsnips.

YUCA TORTILLAS

The starchy tuber yuca is a staple food throughout Latin America, and it adds a distinctive potato-like flavor and texture when worked into a tortilla. These are great with seafood when they're fresh, but they make incredible chips, too—leave them out to go stale for a day and then fry them in oil.

MAKES 12 TORTILLAS

10 ounces fresh masa, or 1 cup masa harina kneaded with ⅔ cup water

1 small yuca, peeled and finely grated (about 6 ounces)

Place the masa and grated yuca in a large bowl and knead gently until the yuca is evenly distributed throughout.

INSPECT THE DOUGH: You want the texture to be as soft and moist as possible without sticking to your hands. If the dough develops small cracks when squeezed, it is too dry and needs more moisture. To correct this, knead water into the dough in 1 tablespoon increments until it becomes malleable and forms into a ball. Cover the dough with a damp towel.

Follow the instructions on pages 35–36 to press and cook the tortillas.

SWEET CORN TORTILLAS

You already know that the sweet corn we eat at barbecues in the United States has little in common with the dense, dry field corn that constitutes masa. The idea of combining the two in a tortilla is really interesting—pitting the toasted grain flavor of one against the raw, sunny sweetness of the other. To make this work you need to chop the raw kernels as fine as possible, until they are almost pulpy, so that they can really fuse with the masa.

Eat these tortillas with summer vegetables like the tomatoes in Pico de Gallo Tacos (page 190); slather them with honey and butter like cornbread; or top with mayonnaise, crumbled Cotija cheese, lime juice, and chile powder for a take on esquites.

MAKES 12 TORTILLAS

½ pound fresh masa, or ¾ cup masa harina kneaded with ½ cup water

3 ears sweet corn, shucked, kernels cut off the cob, finely chopped, and squeezed dry (½ pound)

Place the masa and chopped corn in a large bowl and knead gently until the kernels are evenly distributed throughout.

INSPECT THE DOUGH: You want the texture to be as soft and moist as possible without sticking to your hands. If the dough develops small cracks when squeezed, it is too dry and needs more moisture. To correct this, knead water into the dough in 1 tablespoon increments until it becomes malleable and forms into a ball. Cover the dough with a damp towel.

Follow the instructions on pages 35–36 to press and cook the tortillas.

TORTILLAS STRETCHED WITH ANIMAL PROTEINS

Processing masa with meat that's been ground to the point of creaminess makes for some really intriguing tortillas. More than any of the other neo-traditional recipes we've explored, these really start to shift the mentality about the role tortillas can play in a meal. Taste a tortilla that's saturated with the richness of red chorizo, and you start to wonder whether it's really a canvas for other fillings or a dish unto itself. We focus on poultry and pork here, but this technique would lend itself beautifully to fish, too— think of a salt cod tortilla topped with crushed garlicky potatoes, like a deconstructed brandade. Note that all of these tortillas use a base of dry masa harina. The moisture present in the protein, along with some water added during processing, is enough to hydrate the flour.

CHORIZO TORTILLAS

Give red chorizo some space to stretch out in a masa dough and suddenly all that warm spice, roasted garlic, and the berry tang of guajillo chiles start to magnify. The sausage adds incredible depth of flavor here, and it also transforms the tortilla's texture, making it pliable but also almost cakelike. These are simply awesome—on their own, with scrambled eggs in Breakfast Tacos (page 214), or fried into a kind of alpha-Dorito.

MAKES 12 TORTILLAS

1 cup Red Chorizo (page 228)

1½ cups masa harina

1 teaspoon kosher salt

Add the chorizo to the bowl of a food processor. Add the masa harina, salt, and 2 tablespoons of water and process until smooth.

Transfer the dough to a large bowl and knead gently until smooth and homogenous with a consistent orange color.

INSPECT THE DOUGH: You want the texture to be as soft and moist as possible without sticking to your hands. If the dough develops small cracks when squeezed, it is too dry and needs more moisture. To correct this, knead water into the dough in 1 tablespoon increments until it becomes malleable and forms into a ball. Cover the dough with a damp towel.

Follow the instructions on pages 35–36 to press and cook the tortillas.

CHICKEN TORTILLAS

It was really Mole Poblano (page 100) that inspired this tortilla. I was attached to the idea of including a mole recipe in this book, but I couldn't find the right taco to pair it with. Reducing such a complex, labor-intensive sauce to a garnish felt wrong and disconnected from the way it is often served in Mexico—in a big bowl with simply poached poultry or venison. The challenge was to find a way to make the sauce itself the focal point of a taco. This dense, meaty tortilla, with chicken blended into masa like a Mexican forcemeat, was the solution. A stack of these tortillas splattered with mole and toasted sesame seeds is a delicious way to get the point across.

MAKES 12 TORTILLAS

---

6 ounces raw boneless, skinless chicken breast, cut into small chunks

1½ cups masa harina

1 tablespoon kosher salt

In the bowl of a food processor, combine the chicken, masa harina, salt, and ¾ cup of water and process until smooth.

Transfer the dough to a large bowl and knead gently until smooth and homogenous with a consistent color.

INSPECT THE DOUGH: You want the texture to be as soft and moist as possible without sticking to your hands. If the dough develops small cracks when squeezed, it is too dry and needs more moisture. To correct this, knead water into the dough in 1 tablespoon increments until it becomes malleable and forms into a ball. Cover the dough with a damp towel.

Follow the instructions on pages 35–36 to press and cook the tortillas.

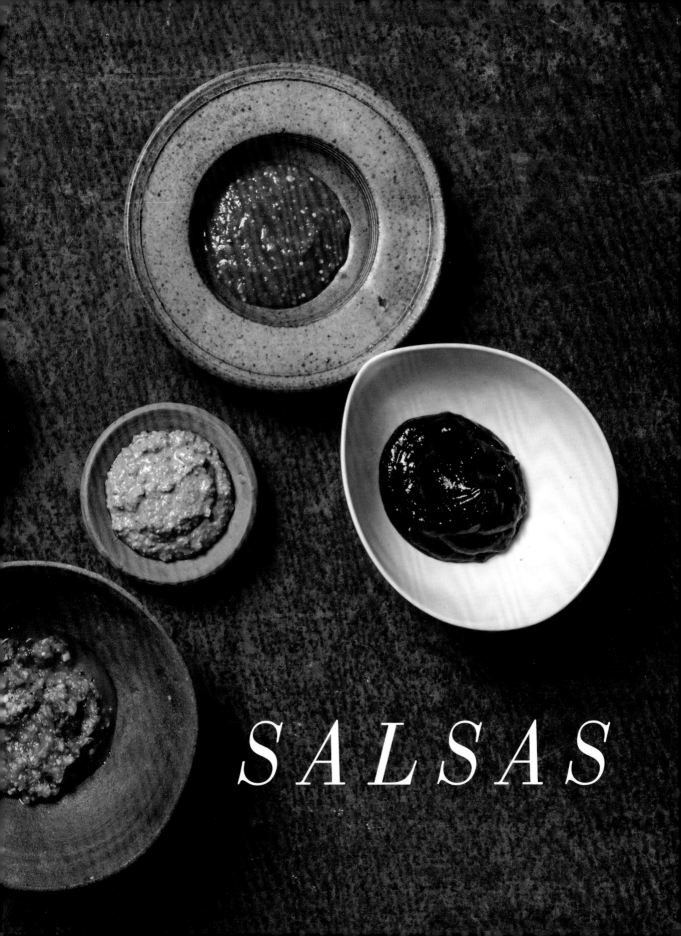

SALSAS

Salsas are the coup de grâce of taco making—the final, decisive flourish that can reinforce or divert the nature of a filling. Reach for a chipotle salsa, and its smoky purr will tease depth from a filling of long-simmered meat; choose a fresh green chile salsa, and the same taco can transform into a bright and brisk thing, dazzling with vegetal flavor.

But wrapping one's head around the vast world of salsas can be a challenge. There's something painterly about it: Just as an artist blends primary colors to yield violet or turquoise, salsas are sprung from the same palette of basic ingredients that have been mixed and manipulated in diverse ways. The ingredients can seem redundant—tomatillos, tomatoes, chiles, onions—but the treatment and proportion of each can dramatically change the end result. Is your fruit raw or roasted? Is the onion minced or sliced? Are the chiles fresh or dried, seeded or left whole? Understand the effects of these technical fluctuations and you'll break through the creative levee—that's what this chapter is all about.

We've broken these salsas into five categories, named for the primary ingredients: salsas based on fresh chiles, dried chiles, tomatoes, tomatillos, or nuts and seeds. Most of the recipes in this chapter match up with a taco presented later in the book, but they stand beautifully on their own too, paired with a basket of tortilla chips or drizzled over roasted meats. As you work through these recipes, I hope you'll accumulate an arsenal of techniques that can be applied to other salsas in the book or be used as a jumping-off point to create your own fiery compounds. The recipes accelerate in complexity, culminating in a classic Mole Poblano—that rabbit hole of a Mexican sauce with its almanac of ingredients and labyrinthine preparation. By the time you arrive at the mole threshold, though, you'll be armed with the knowledge to take it on.

Note that some of these salsas call for use of a molcajete and tejolote, the traditional Mesoamerican basalt stone mortar and pestle. (You've probably seen this used to make tableside guacamole in the United States. Don't even get me started.) Using a molcajete to grind salsa will give you more control over its texture—a coarse, pulpy consistency is easier to achieve by hand. A blender will yield a more uniform salsa, but it's a fine solution if you don't have a molcajete.

FRESH CHILE SALSAS

The fruity, grassy, and vegetal notes of fresh chiles make for some of the most intoxicating salsas on earth. They taste pure, vivid, and alive with a flavor you just cannot capture by working with dried chiles. But they're also, by design, blindingly spicy. Whereas other styles of salsa are cut with tomato or tomatillo to mitigate the pepper's brutal heat, these variants typically feature just the chile itself, flavored with garlic or onion and spices. Fresh chile salsas work well on their own, or you can use them to alter heat levels in other condiments.

SALSA ARRIERA

One of the most compelling things about salsas is their infinite range. They can be thick and intense with long-simmered flavor, as aggressive as a doom-metal lyric. Or they can be quick and wicked, like this salsa arriera—a simple grind of blistered serrano chiles with aromatics. Few ingredients and a straightforward method make this a good foundational salsa, showcasing the serrano's fierce heat and green pepper flavor.

MAKES ABOUT 1 CUP

3 garlic cloves, skins on

15 serrano chiles

1½ teaspoons kosher salt

½ medium white onion, minced

EQUIPMENT: Molcajete*

*If you don't have a molcajete, prep all of the ingredients as instructed and add them all at once to the jar of a blender. Pulse to combine and season with salt.

Set a 12-inch cast-iron skillet over medium heat for 5 minutes. Add the garlic and chiles and roast, turning them from time to time, until softened slightly and blackened in spots, about 6 minutes. Turn off the heat, remove the vegetables from the skillet, and set aside to cool at room temperature. Once they are cool enough to handle, peel the garlic and discard the skins.

Place the roasted garlic into the molcajete with 1 teaspoon of the salt and crush to a paste using the tejolote. Add the minced onion and crush until coarse.

Remove and discard the stems of the roasted chiles and cut into quarters lengthwise. Roughly chop the chiles and add to the molcajete, followed by 5 tablespoons water. Continue working the salsa to a coarse texture.

Season with the remaining ½ teaspoon salt and stir to combine. Transfer to a container, or refrigerate until ready to use. The salsa will keep for up to 3 days.

SALSA HABANERA

The habanero chile is a tricky little siren. Give the pepper a sniff as it chars in a skillet, and it's all passionfruit, guava, and fresh-cut grass. Bite into it, and you'll enjoy a few seconds of those flavors before the heat locks its jaw around your tongue. To love the habanero is to be in constant pursuit of those opiate moments just before the capsaicin rolls in. Tropical fruit and old-growth pastures—nothing in the world tastes so beautiful and is so ephemeral. When working the habanero into a salsa, I like to get out of its way—add some simple aromatics and sweet citrus, then let the pepper do its thing.

If you're using a molcajete for this salsa, note that the habanero skin becomes leathery when roasted, so grinding the salsa takes some elbow grease.

MAKES ABOUT 1 CUP

½ teaspoon dried Mexican oregano

10 habanero chiles

½ medium white onion, cut into ¼-inch-thick slices

1 teaspoon kosher salt

1 tablespoon sugar

1 orange, juiced and zest finely grated

1 lime, juiced and zest finely grated

1 tablespoon cider vinegar

EQUIPMENT: Molcajete*

*If you don't have a molcajete, prep all of the ingredients as instructed and add them all at once to the jar of a blender. Pulse to combine and season with salt.

Set a 12-inch cast-iron skillet over medium heat for 5 minutes. Add the oregano and toast briefly, shaking the pan until fragrant, about 15 seconds. Remove from the heat and transfer to a molcajete.

Roast the habanero chiles in the hot skillet, turning them from time to time, until blackened in spots, about 15 minutes. Remove from the skillet and set aside to cool to room temperature.

Add the onion slices to the skillet and roast, turning them from time to time, until softened slightly and blackened in spots, about 6 minutes. Remove from the skillet and set aside to cool to room temperature.

Roughly chop the roasted onion and add to the molcajete along with the salt and sugar. Using the tejolote, crush into a paste.

Remove and discard the stems of the roasted chiles and cut into quarters lengthwise. Roughly chop the chiles and add to the molcajete, followed by the orange and lime zest and juices. Continue working the salsa to a coarse texture.

Stir in the cider vinegar. Transfer to a container, or refrigerate until ready to use. The salsa will keep for up to 3 days.

DRIED CHILE SALSAS

The flavor of dried chiles is inimitable; instead of the brightness of fresh peppers, you get that deep, rusty intensity so fundamental to Mexican cuisine. Before incorporating a dried chile into a salsa, you need to apply heat (via toasting or frying) to develop its aroma. And then you need to soak the chiles, too: Plump them in water as you would for a salsa roja, and you'll curb the spiciness; submerge them in piloncillo syrup, and you'll bring out their sweetness, as in a salsa negra.

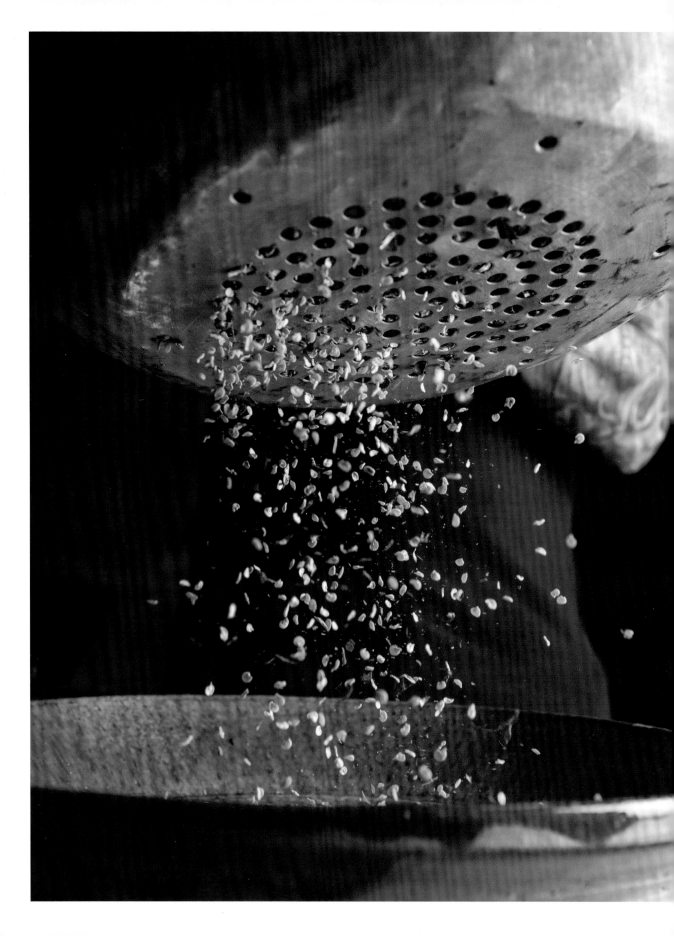

SALSA DE ÁRBOL

Hot sauces tend to inspire a kind of tribal devotion—you definitely know a chile head with sworn fealty to Sriracha, Tabasco, Crystal, or Frank's RedHot. If I had to carry a banner, I'd choose this salsa de árbol, a jaw-rattling chord of stiff heat and winter spice enriched with seeds. The vinegar content keeps the salsa preserved, so you can store it in the fridge for a long time, right next to the Cholula.

MAKES ABOUT 1½ CUPS

⅛ teaspoon cumin seeds

6 allspice berries

3 whole cloves

½ teaspoon dried Mexican oregano

40 árbol chiles

4 garlic cloves, skins on

¼ cup hulled sesame seeds

¼ cup raw, hulled, unsalted pepitas (pumpkin seeds)

1 teaspoon kosher salt

1 tablespoon sugar

1 cup cider vinegar

Set a 12-inch cast-iron skillet over medium heat for 5 minutes. Add the cumin seeds, allspice berries, whole cloves, and oregano and toast briefly, shaking the pan until fragrant, about 15 seconds. Remove from the heat, transfer to a spice grinder, and grind to a fine powder. Transfer to a bowl.

Remove the stems from the árbol chiles. Place the chiles in a food processor and pulse two or three times to break them open. Transfer the chile pieces to a colander to sift out the seeds. Discard the seeds.

Reheat the skillet over medium heat. Add the chile pieces and toast, shaking the pan from time to time, until you see the first wisp of smoke, about 30 seconds. Remove pan from heat, and transfer the chiles to a bowl. Cover them with hot tap water and place a heavy plate over the chiles to keep them submerged. Set aside to soak for 30 minutes.

Add the garlic cloves to the skillet and roast, turning them from time to time, until softened slightly and blackened in spots, about 6 minutes. Remove the garlic from the skillet and set aside to cool at room temperature. Once they are cool enough to handle, peel the garlic cloves and discard the skins.

Next, toast the sesame seeds in the skillet until dark golden brown, shaking the pan constantly to prevent them from burning, about 15 seconds. Remove from the heat and transfer to the bowl with the ground spices.

Finally, toast the pepitas until golden, shaking the pan constantly, 2 to 3 minutes. Remove from the heat and reserve with the spices and sesame seeds.

Drain the soaked chiles and discard the liquid. Place them in a blender along with the roasted garlic, toasted spices, sesame seeds, pepitas, and the salt, sugar, and cider vinegar. Puree on high speed until completely smooth, working in batches if necessary. Set up a medium-mesh sieve over a bowl and pass the puree through the strainer. Transfer to a container, or refrigerate until ready to use. The salsa will keep for up to 1 month.

SALSA NEGRA

This is one of those oddball salsas you'll make, stick in the refrigerator, and forget about—that is, until one hungover Sunday morning, when you're cooking bacon and the memory of its smoldering molasses funk lights up your brain. Negra is a specialty of Carmen Ramírez Degollado, of the El Bajío restaurants in Mexico City, where it is used as a condiment for black bean gorditas and carnitas. But the flavor of smoke-dried chipotle morita chiles plumped in sweet piloncillo syrup can go toe-to-toe with any American barbecue sauce.

Negra utilizes a uniquely Mexican technique of literally "frying" the salsa in ripping-hot fat until it takes on the color and texture of tar. It's a sputtery, unfamiliar method, but well worth doing; use a high-walled pan to protect yourself from burns as the sauce bubbles and reduces.

MAKES ABOUT 2 CUPS

One 8-ounce cone piloncillo

6 garlic cloves, skins on

½ cup plus 1 teaspoon lard or vegetable oil

60 chipotle morita chiles, stemmed

1 teaspoon kosher salt

Place the piloncillo and 2 cups water in a 2-quart nonreactive saucepan and set over high heat. Bring the mixture to a rolling boil and immediately remove from the heat. Let the piloncillo dissolve, using a wooden spoon to help break it up as it softens.

Set a 12-inch cast-iron skillet over medium heat for 5 minutes. Add the garlic cloves and roast, turning them from time to time until softened slightly and blackened in spots, about 6 minutes. Remove the garlic from the skillet and set aside to cool. Once they are cool enough to handle, peel the garlic cloves and discard the skins.

Add ½ cup of the lard to the skillet and heat until shimmering. Working in batches, fry the chiles for about 30 seconds. Remove the pan from the heat, and using a slotted spoon, transfer the chipotles to the piloncillo syrup. Place a heavy plate over the chiles to keep them submerged. Soak for 30 minutes.

Place the soaked chiles in a blender along with the piloncillo syrup and the roasted garlic. Puree on high speed until completely smooth, working in batches if necessary. Set aside.

Set a 4-quart nonreactive saucepan over medium heat. Add the remaining teaspoon of lard and heat until smoking. Pour in the chile puree all at once (the puree will sputter) and sear for 1 minute. Lower the heat to a simmer and stir with a wooden spoon. Continue stirring as you cook the puree down to a thick, dark paste, about 10 minutes. Be careful as you stir; the puree will continue to sputter as it reduces.

Season the negra with the salt and continue to cook for 3 more minutes. Remove from the heat and let cool to room temperature; it will continue to thicken as it cools. Transfer to a container and refrigerate until ready to use. The salsa will keep for up to 1 month.

SALSA ROJA

Salsa roja and salsa verde (see page 77) are the ebony and ivory of the salsa universe: Whereas verde supplies brightness and clean, sharp heat, roja offers gentle spice and dried-herb warmth. It makes sense that the two keep such close company—you'll encounter versions of both at nearly every taqueria in Mexico.

For my salsa roja, I looked to guajillo chile, one of the workhorses of the Mexican pantry. Cheap and ubiquitous, these dried peppers impart the mild heat, distinctive berry-like aroma, and deep, rusty hue that define a good roja.

MAKES ABOUT 2 CUPS

---

2 plum tomatoes

10 guajillo chiles

1 chipotle morita chile

½ teaspoon dried Mexican oregano

⅛ teaspoon cumin seeds

5 garlic cloves, skins on

1½ teaspoons kosher salt

1 tablespoon sugar

1 tablespoon cider vinegar

Preheat the broiler. Roast the tomatoes on a baking sheet under the broiler until blackened in spots, about 7 minutes. Turn them over and continue to blacken, about another 7 minutes. Remove from the broiler and set aside to cool at room temperature. Once they are cool enough to handle, peel the tomatoes and discard the skins.

Remove the stems from the guajillo and chipotle chiles and tear them open. Shake out and discard the seeds. Remove and discard the veins.

Set a 12-inch cast-iron skillet over medium heat for 5 minutes. Add the oregano and cumin seeds and toast briefly, shaking the pan, until fragrant, about 15 seconds. Remove from the heat, transfer to a spice grinder, and grind to a fine powder.

Reheat the skillet over medium heat. Toast the guajillo and chipotle chiles, turning them from time to time until you see the first wisp of smoke, about 45 seconds.

Remove pan from heat, and transfer the chiles to a bowl. Cover them with hot tap water and place a heavy plate over the chiles to keep them submerged. Set aside to soak for 30 minutes.

Add the garlic cloves to the skillet and roast, turning them from time to time until softened slightly and blackened in spots, about 6 minutes. Turn off the heat, remove the garlic from the skillet, and set aside to cool at room temperature. Once they are cool enough to handle, peel the garlic cloves and discard the skins.

Drain the soaked chiles and discard the liquid. Place them in a blender along with the ground spices and roasted garlic, the salt, sugar, cider vinegar, and ¼ cup water. Puree on high speed until completely smooth, working in batches if necessary. Set up a medium-mesh sieve over a bowl and pass the puree through the strainer. Transfer to a container or refrigerate until ready to use. The salsa will keep for up to 3 days.

TOMATO-BASED SALSAS

The salsas in this section are designed to show off the range of a common tomato, from the subtle sweetness and acid of the fruit in its raw state to the rich aroma it takes on when roasted. Charred, blistered tomatoes are something of a benchmark flavor in this cuisine—it's that cinder-like perfume that starts to make a tomato sauce taste Mexican and not, say, like an Italian marinara. Of course the chile heat helps, too, and tomato-based salsas are perfect for cooks who like to customize their burn. Unlike chile salsas, which are unilaterally spicy, tomato salsas can be modified to be as mild or potent as you wish.

SALSA MEXICANA

"Pico de gallo" can mean a lot of things in Mexico. In Oaxaca, pico can be a grapefruit salad with chiles and honey. In other regions, it refers generally to a fresh fruit salsa. In the United States, though, *pico de gallo* is shorthand for what is ubiquitously known south of the border as salsa Mexicana: a chop of fresh tomato, jalapeño or serrano chile, cilantro, and onion. Browse enough Mexican menus and you'll start to notice that anything served "a la Mexicana" arrives smothered in these red, white, and green ingredients—a bit of gastro-patriotism that gives a nod to the colors of the Mexican flag.

This salsa is delicious raw, but you can also cook it down and use it as an aromatic base for other dishes.

MAKES ABOUT 2 CUPS

3 plum tomatoes, diced

2 serrano chiles, stemmed and finely chopped

1 garlic clove, minced

½ medium white onion, minced

1 lime

1 teaspoon kosher salt

40 cilantro leaves (from about 10 sprigs), roughly chopped

In a large bowl, combine the tomatoes, chiles, garlic, and onion. Cut the lime in half and squeeze the juice directly over a medium-mesh strainer (to catch any seeds) into the bowl.

Season the salsa with salt. Add the chopped cilantro and stir to combine. Transfer to a container and refrigerate until ready to use. Salsa Mexicana doesn't keep well—eat it the day it is made.

XNI PEC

Raw, Yucatecan xni pec is essentially a salsa Mexicana with some regional variations: crisp radishes, red onion instead of white, and habanero, the chile of the Yucatán, instead of serrano. Sour orange is very common on the southeastern peninsula, so I call for it here: the fruit adds acid and a singular incense-like note similar to bergamot, but lime will do in a pinch. I've heard that the Mayan translation of *xni pec* is "dog's nose," named for the way the habanero heat can make your nose run. It'll certainly make your eyes water—take care to finely mince the chile so no one gets bushwacked by a potent chunk of it.

MAKES ABOUT 2½ CUPS

---

2 plum tomatoes, diced

½ habanero chile, stemmed, seeded, and finely chopped

5 small radishes, cut into matchsticks

½ medium red onion, minced

1 sour orange (substitute a lime if you can't find this fruit)

1 teaspoon kosher salt

40 cilantro leaves (from about 10 sprigs), roughly chopped

In a large bowl, combine the tomatoes, chile, radishes, and red onion. Cut the sour orange in half and squeeze the juice directly over a medium-mesh strainer (to catch any seeds) into the bowl. Season with salt, add the chopped cilantro to the bowl, and stir to combine. Transfer to a container and refrigerate until ready to use. Xni pec doesn't keep well—eat it the day it is made.

SALSA RANCHERA

Judged by its ingredients alone, there isn't much to distinguish this chunky salsa—an essential condiment for huevos rancheros—from a rustic Italian tomato sauce. In Italy, you might find chile flakes adding the heat instead of a serrano, or basil standing in for the epazote. But with so many parallels, salsa ranchera really helps illuminate what makes something taste uniquely Mexican. Roasting the garlic cloves and tomatoes in their skins to impart that smoky perfume; cooking down the puree in a skillet shimmering with hot lard—these are the kinds of subtle calibrations that mark the Mexican culinary vernacular, and you'll encounter them again and again as you make the salsas in this book.

MAKES ABOUT 1½ CUPS

5 plum tomatoes

3 garlic cloves, skins on

2 serrano chiles

2 tablespoons lard or vegetable oil

½ medium white onion, minced

1 cup Chicken Broth (page 230) or water

1 epazote branch

1 tablespoon kosher salt

Preheat the broiler. Roast the tomatoes on a baking sheet under the broiler until blackened in spots, about 7 minutes. Turn them over and continue to blacken, another 7 minutes. Remove from the broiler and set aside to cool at room temperature. Once they are cool enough to handle, peel the tomatoes and discard the skins.

Set a 12-inch cast-iron skillet over medium heat for 5 minutes. Add the garlic cloves and serrano chiles and roast, turning them from time to time until softened slightly and blackened in spots, about 6 minutes. Turn off the heat, remove the vegetables from the skillet, and set aside to cool at room temperature. Once they are cool enough to handle, peel the garlic cloves and discard the skins. Remove and discard the stems and seeds of the chiles.

Place the roasted tomatoes in a blender, followed by the roasted chiles and garlic; pulse until pulpy.

Place a 4-quart nonreactive saucepan over medium heat. Add the lard and heat until shimmering. Add the onion and cook until lightly browned. Pour in the tomato puree, bring to a boil, and cook until reduced by half, about 6 minutes.

Add the broth, epazote, and salt and bring to a simmer. Cook until the sauce clings to the back of a spoon, about 10 minutes. Remove from the heat and let cool to room temperature. Transfer to a container and refrigerate until ready to use. The salsa will keep for up to 1 week.

SALSA VERACRUZ

The Spanish influence on Mexican cuisine is keenly felt in Veracruz, the eastern state where European conquistador Hernán Cortés made landfall in the sixteenth century. You can sense it all over the region—in the olives, garlic, oil, capers, and other continental ingredients mingling with the area's incomparable seafood. This salsa functions as a kind of edible scrapbook of the cultural history of Veracruz: Spanish ingredients mixing with Moorish cinnamon and native Mexican chiles. It's common to find whole fish steam-baked in this mellow, brothy sauce, but the sauce is also perfect as a cool condiment, spooned over meat or seafood.

MAKES ABOUT 4 CUPS

¼ teaspoon dried marjoram

¼ teaspoon dried thyme

One 1-inch stick of canela (Mexican cinnamon)

3 whole cloves

½ teaspoon black peppercorns

2 tablespoons extra-virgin olive oil

½ medium white onion, minced

2 garlic cloves, minced

5 plum tomatoes, diced

20 manzanilla olives, pitted and minced

2 tablespoons brined capers, drained and minced

2 Pickled Jalapeños (page 231), diced

1 cup Fish Broth (page 231) or water

1 dried bay leaf

1 teaspoon kosher salt

40 parsley leaves (from about 8 sprigs), roughly chopped

Set a 12-inch cast-iron skillet over medium heat for 5 minutes. Add the marjoram, thyme, canela, cloves, and peppercorns; toast, shaking the pan, until fragrant, about 15 seconds. Remove from the heat, transfer the spices to a spice grinder, and grind to a fine powder.

Place a 4-quart nonreactive saucepan over medium heat. Add the olive oil and heat until shimmering. Add the onion and sweat until translucent, about 3 minutes. Add the garlic and cook for about 1 minute, making sure it does not brown.

Add the tomatoes, olives, capers, jalapeños, broth, bay leaf, and ground spices to the saucepan. Lower the heat to a simmer and cook the sauce to a light, brothy consistency, about 7 minutes. Season with the salt and stir in the chopped parsley. Remove from the heat and let cool to room temperature. Transfer to a container and refrigerate until ready to use. The salsa will keep for up to 1 week.

TINGA POBLANA

Tinga Poblana is sort of the Pueblan equivalent of Italian Sunday gravy: a flexible meat sauce made with chorizo and roasted tomato, spiced with chipotle peppers and bulked up with whatever is on hand—zucchini, pumpkin, and chicken are common. The first time I made this salsa, I instantly thought of my father, Al Stupak, and his pasta sauce—a jar of canned marinara, a pound of ground hamburger, and boom: gravy. With lots of toasted herbs and intensely spiced red chorizo, my tinga has more going on than my dad's meat sauce. But it tastes just as good when dressing a tortilla as it would on a pile of spaghetti.

MAKES ABOUT 2 CUPS

5 plum tomatoes

¼ teaspoon dried marjoram

¼ teaspoon dried Mexican oregano

1 dried bay leaf

2 garlic cloves, skins on

1 tablespoon lard or vegetable oil

½ medium white onion, minced

½ pound Red Chorizo (page 228)

2 canned chipotle chiles, minced

1 teaspoon kosher salt

1 teaspoon sugar

RED CHORIZO

Preheat the broiler. Roast the tomatoes on a baking sheet under the broiler until blackened in spots, about 7 minutes. Turn them over and continue to blacken, another 7 minutes. Remove from the broiler and set aside to cool at room temperature. Once they are cool enough to handle, peel the tomatoes and discard the skins.

Set a 12-inch cast-iron skillet over medium heat for 5 minutes. Add the marjoram, oregano, and bay leaf and toast until fragrant, about 15 seconds. Remove from the heat, transfer to a spice grinder, and grind to a fine powder. Transfer to a bowl.

Reheat the skillet over medium heat. Add the garlic cloves and roast, turning them from time to time, until softened slightly and blackened in spots, about 6 minutes. Turn off the heat, remove the garlic from the skillet, and set aside to cool at room temperature. Once they are cool enough to handle, peel the garlic cloves and discard the skins.

Place the roasted tomatoes and roasted garlic in a blender and puree on high speed until completely smooth. Set up a medium-mesh sieve over a bowl and pass the puree through the strainer. Set aside.

Place a 4-quart nonreactive saucepan over medium heat. Add the lard and heat until shimmering. Add the onion and cook until lightly browned. Add the chorizo to the saucepan and cook until crumbly, about 8 minutes, then stir in the chipotle chiles, followed by the tomato puree and the ground herbs.

Season the tinga with the salt and sugar, and cook until the liquid is reduced by half, about 8 minutes. Remove from the heat and let cool to room temperature. Transfer to a container and refrigerate until ready to use. Refrigerated, the salsa will keep for a week, or you can freeze it for up to 1 month.

TOMATILLO-BASED SALSAS

The first thing you need to know about tomatillos is that if you ask for them in a Mexican market, you'll be greeted with a shrug; in Mexico, they're called tomates verdes. Whatever you choose to call it, the tomatillo is one of those irrefutably Mexican ingredients that hasn't had much traction in other international cuisines. But the vibrant fruit—a member of the gooseberry family, with an astringent flavor that smacks of green apple skin—offers an awful lot of latitude in salsas. In this section we look at a variety of ways to treat the tomatillo and how it behaves differently when it's highly manipulated or left to speak for itself. Along with three approaches to a salsa verde (boiling the fruit, roasting it, or leaving it raw), we've included recipes that showcase the tomatillo as a foil for deeper, more matured flavors: the spice-box intensity of a mole verde and the smoky heft of a tomatillo-chipotle salsa.

SALSA BORRACHA

BOILED SALSA VERDE

RAW SALSA VERDE

ROASTED SALSA VERDE

3 VARIATIONS ON *SALSA VERDE*

Salsa verde is the go-to table salsa throughout Mexico, regardless of region, and it's as ubiquitous as ketchup is in the United States. In fact, that's a fair comparison as condiments go. For Americans, the right to treasure Heinz is inalienable; it's a sweet, tart, vaguely spiced flavor that can keep balance on the tines of a fork. Salsa verde has those qualities, too: That tomatillo astringency, with a bit of background sugar, tempers the savory cilantro and chile tingle. Rare is the taco that's not improved with a spoonful of the stuff—and in Mexico, it's never far from reach.

Because the ingredients for a classic salsa verde are so simple, it presents a great opportunity to illustrate the alchemy at play in Mexican kitchens. There's no better way to understand the transformative effect of manipulating ingredients than a side-by-side tasting of the three recipes that follow. It's also a chance to explore how your personal taste translates to Mexican food. Do you like the lip-singeing brightness of a raw salsa verde? The mature intensity that develops when you roast the ingredients? Or the mellow cohesion of a boiled salsa?

We use the same proportions for all three versions to keep the comparison tidy. Note that the cilantro is the least shelf-stable ingredient in a salsa verde; you can make these salsas up to three days in advance if you wait to incorporate the herb until you're just about to serve.

RAW SALSA VERDE

Raw ingredients speak (shout, actually) for themselves in this purist salsa verde. It's all about the green apple acidity of ripe tomatillo, the heat of untreated chiles, and the garlicky sting right up front.

MAKES ABOUT 1 CUP

---

1 garlic clove, roughly chopped

1 teaspoon kosher salt

2 serrano chiles, stemmed and roughly chopped

½ medium white onion, minced

3-4 medium tomatillos (about 5 ounces total), husked, rinsed, patted dry, and diced

1 teaspoon honey

40 cilantro leaves (from about 10 sprigs), roughly chopped

EQUIPMENT: Molcajete*

*If you don't have a molcajete, prep all the ingredients as instructed and add them, minus the cilantro, at once to the jar of a blender. Pulse to combine then stir in the chopped cilantro.

Place the garlic in the molcajete with the salt and crush to a paste using the tejolote.

Add the chiles and minced onion to the paste and crush to a coarse texture. Add the tomatillos and continue crushing with the tejolote until pulpy. Season with the honey and stir with a spoon. Add the chopped cilantro and stir to combine. Transfer to a container and refrigerate until ready to use. The finished salsa is best eaten the day it is made; if you want to work ahead, don't add the cilantro to the salsa until the day you plan to serve it.

BOILED SALSA VERDE

If raw salsa verde is the boldest of the bunch, the boiled version is the most demure. Simmering the ingredients gives this salsa a smooth consistency and a cohesive flavor. It also tones down the spice, making it ideal for diners who prefer a more mild heat.

MAKES ABOUT 1 CUP

3-4 medium tomatillos (about 5 ounces total), husked, rinsed, and patted dry

1 garlic clove, peeled

2 serrano chiles, stemmed and cut in half lengthwise

½ medium white onion, cut into large chunks

1 teaspoon kosher salt

1 teaspoon honey

40 cilantro leaves (from about 10 sprigs), roughly chopped

Place the tomatillos, garlic, chiles, and onion in a 2-quart nonreactive saucepan. Cover with cold water and bring to a boil over medium heat. Lower the heat to a simmer and cook until the tomatillos soften and turn a dull army green, about 7 minutes.

Remove the saucepan from the heat. Strain out the water and transfer the vegetables to a plate to cool at room temperature.

Place the tomatillo mixture in a blender along with the salt and honey. Puree on high speed until coarse. Transfer to a container, add the cilantro, and stir to combine. Refrigerate until ready to use. The finished salsa is best eaten the day it is made; if you want to work ahead, don't add the cilantro to the salsa until the day you plan to serve it.

ROASTED SALSA VERDE

If I had to choose just one salsa verde to eat in perpetuity, it would be this one. In a sense, it splits the difference between its raw and boiled brethren: Roasting the ingredients takes the edge off a bit, but it also deepens the flavors in a remarkable way. Suddenly, those tomatillos are behaving like warm fruit—they even release their own sweet caramel as the broiler heat draws their sugar to the surface. (Drag a spoon through this stuff and lick it; it tastes like Werther's on a juice cleanse.)

MAKES ABOUT 1 CUP

3-4 medium tomatillos (about 5 ounces total), husked, rinsed, and patted dry

1 garlic clove, skin on

½ medium white onion, cut into ¼-inch-thick slices

2 serrano chiles

1 teaspoon kosher salt, plus more as needed

1 teaspoon honey

40 cilantro leaves (from about 10 sprigs), roughly chopped

EQUIPMENT: Molcajete*

*If you don't have a molcajete, prep all of the ingredients as instructed and add them, minus the cilantro, all at once to the jar of a blender. Pulse to combine and then stir in the cilantro.

Preheat the broiler. Roast the tomatillos on a baking sheet under the broiler until blackened in spots, about 7 minutes. Turn them over and continue to blacken, another 7 minutes. Remove from the broiler and set aside to cool at room temperature.

Set a 12-inch cast-iron skillet over medium heat for 5 minutes. Add the garlic, onion slices, and chiles and roast, turning them from time to time, until softened slightly and blackened in spots, about 6 minutes. Turn off the heat, remove the vegetables from the skillet, and set aside to cool at room temperature. Once they are cool enough to handle, peel the garlic clove and discard the skin. Remove and discard the stems of the chiles. Set aside.

Place the roasted garlic in the molcajete with 1 teaspoon salt and crush to a paste using the tejolote.

Roughly chop the roasted onion, add to the molcajete, and continue crushing to a coarse texture.

Dice the roasted tomatillos, add to the molcajete, and continue working the salsa until pulpy. Season with salt and honey and stir with a spoon. Add the chopped cilantro and stir to combine. Transfer to a container and refrigerate until ready to use. The finished salsa is best eaten the day it is made; if you want to work ahead, don't add the cilantro to the salsa until the day you plan to serve it.

SALSA BORRACHA

Like a lot of things in Mexican cuisine, the recipe for salsa borracha ("drunken salsa") is a moving target. Every borracha I've encountered contains heat and hooch, but that's the only through line. I've seen them made with different types of chiles (árbols, chipotles, pasillas) and different kinds of booze (tequila, pulque, beer).

To nail down our recipe, I thought about the place I first encountered this salsa: at a lamb barbacoa stand at Central de Abastos market in Oaxaca. It just makes sense to match up two of that region's seminal flavors: roasty mezcal with the campfire smokiness of pasilla Oaxaqueño.

MAKES ABOUT 1¼ CUPS

3-4 medium tomatillos (about 5 ounces total), husked, rinsed, and patted dry

2 pasilla Oaxaqueño chiles

1 garlic clove, skin on

½ medium white onion, cut into ¼-inch-thick slices

1 teaspoon kosher salt

1 teaspoon honey

¼ cup mezcal

Preheat the broiler. Roast the tomatillos on a baking sheet under the broiler until blackened in spots, about 7 minutes. Turn them over and continue to blacken, another 7 minutes. Remove from the broiler and set aside to cool at room temperature.

Remove the stems from the chiles and tear them open. Shake out and discard the seeds. Remove and discard the veins.

Set a 12-inch cast-iron skillet over medium heat for 5 minutes. Add the chiles and toast, turning them from time to time, until you see the first wisp of smoke, about 45 seconds. Remove the pan from the heat, and transfer the chiles to a bowl. Cover them with hot tap water and place a heavy plate over the chiles to keep them submerged. Set aside to soak for 30 minutes.

Reheat the skillet over medium heat. Add the garlic clove and onion slices and roast, turning them from time to time, until softened slightly and blackened in spots, about 6 minutes. Turn off the heat, remove the vegetables from the skillet, and set aside to cool at room temperature. Once it is cool enough to handle, peel the garlic clove and discard the skin.

Drain the soaked chiles and discard the liquid. Place the chiles in a blender along with the roasted tomatillos, garlic, and onion, as well as the salt, honey, and mezcal. Puree on high speed until completely smooth, working in batches if necessary. Set up a medium-mesh sieve over a bowl and pass the puree through the strainer. Transfer to a container and refrigerate until ready to use. The salsa will keep for up to 1 week.

TOMATILLO-CHIPOTLE SALSA

The chromotology of food has always interested me: the way the color of a dish can speak to its flavor, even before you taste it. Caramel hues might call to mind deep savor, while bright greens can suggest clean, vegetal bite. Coming from the world of Alinea and wd~50, I've also thought about color as an opportunity to manipulate the senses and people's expectations—and that's where this salsa comes in. You might expect a tomatillo-based salsa to be fresh and astringent. But this one is the color of rust, and so the flavor of tart green fruit is a surprise.

This is a highly adaptable salsa that takes well to just about any dried chile. The Squash Blossom Tacos (page 199) call for a variation that uses pasillas Oaxaqueños instead of the chipotles. To make the variation, stem, seed, and devein two dried pasillas Oaxaqueños, and then toast and soak them as you would for Salsa Borracha (page 81).

MAKES ABOUT 1 CUP

3-4 medium tomatillos (about 5 ounces total), husked, rinsed, and patted dry

2 garlic cloves, skins on

½ medium white onion, cut into ¼-inch-thick slices

3 canned chipotle chiles

1 teaspoon kosher salt

1 teaspoon honey

Preheat the broiler. Roast the tomatillos on a baking sheet under the broiler until blackened in spots, about 7 minutes. Turn them over and continue to blacken, another 7 minutes. Remove from the broiler and set aside to cool at room temperature.

Set a 12-inch cast-iron skillet over medium heat for 5 minutes. Add the garlic cloves and onion slices and roast, turning them from time to time, until softened slightly and blackened in spots, about 6 minutes. Turn off the heat, remove the vegetables from the skillet, and set aside to cool at room temperature. Once they are cool enough to handle, peel the garlic cloves and discard the skins.

Place the roasted tomatillos in a blender along with the roasted garlic, roasted onion, the chiles, salt, and honey and puree on high speed until coarse, working in batches if necessary. Transfer to a container and refrigerate until ready to use. The salsa will keep for up to 3 days.

CAPE GOOSEBERRY SALSA

Mango and pineapple have their place in Mexican cuisine, but I've never been particularly interested in fruity salsas. They feel dated, like something you'd find topping a canapé at a party in the nineties. Still, experimenting with cape gooseberries—also known as ground cherries—felt intriguing. The tiny orange fruits in the nightshade family are closely related to tomatillos, and they add more sweetness and concentrated tang than their larger cousins. This salsa toys with that natural affinity: It's a variation on the Tomatillo-Chipotle Salsa (opposite), replacing the tomatillos with gooseberries. I like this one best with simple grilled fish.

MAKES ABOUT 1¾ CUPS

---

40 cape gooseberries, husked, rinsed, and patted dry

2 garlic cloves, skins on

½ medium white onion, cut into ¼-inch-thick slices

3 canned chipotle chiles

1 teaspoon kosher salt

1 teaspoon honey

Preheat the broiler. Roast the cape gooseberries on a baking sheet under the broiler until blackened in spots, about 3 minutes. Shake the baking sheet and continue to roast for another 3 minutes. Remove from the broiler and set aside to cool at room temperature.

Set a 12-inch cast-iron skillet over medium heat for 5 minutes. Add the garlic cloves and onion slices and roast, turning them from time to time, until softened slightly and blackened in spots, about 6 minutes. Turn off the heat, remove the vegetables from the skillet, and set aside to cool at room temperature. Once they are cool enough to handle, peel the garlic cloves and discard the skins.

Place the roasted cape gooseberries in a blender along with the roasted garlic and onion, and the chiles, salt, and honey. Puree on high speed until coarse, working in batches if necessary. Transfer to a container and refrigerate until ready to use. The salsa will keep for up to 3 days.

MOLE VERDE

Journalist Calvin Trillin once described the making of mole as "a process so laborious that it puts most complicated Continental dishes into the category of Pop-Tart preparation by comparison." This one doesn't have any of the benchmark components that make classic moles so complex—no fried nuts, dried chiles, or chocolate. Instead, this mole verde is all about bright vegetal and herb flavor, with a thick, almost creamy consistency that's derived from masa. One of the seven moles of Oaxaca, it's often served like a soup, with pork and chochoyones (masa dumplings) floating inside. Mole verde's green chile heat and vivid cilantro, parsley, and epazote punch make it an able match for the Pork Rind Tacos (page 136).

MAKES ABOUT 4 CUPS

7-9 medium tomatillos (about ¾ pound total), husked, rinsed, and patted dry

½ teaspoon black peppercorns

8 whole cloves

¼ teaspoon cumin seeds

8 garlic cloves, skins on

½ medium white onion, cut into ¼-inch-thick slices

3 serrano chiles

2 cups Chicken Broth (page 230) or water

½ pound fresh masa, or 6 tablespoons masa harina

60 cilantro leaves (from about 15 sprigs)

60 parsley leaves (from about 12 sprigs)

30 epazote leaves (from about 6 branches)

1 leaf hoja santa

2 tablespoons lard or vegetable oil

2 tablespoons kosher salt

1 tablespoon sugar

Preheat the broiler. Roast the tomatillos on a baking sheet under the broiler until blackened in spots, about 7 minutes. Turn them over and continue to blacken, another 7 minutes. Remove from the broiler and set aside to cool at room temperature.

Set a 12-inch cast-iron skillet over medium heat for 5 minutes. Add the peppercorns, cloves, and cumin seeds and toast, shaking the pan, until fragrant, about 15 seconds. Remove from the heat, transfer to a spice grinder, and grind to a fine powder.

Reheat the skillet over medium heat. Add the garlic cloves, onion slices, and serrano chiles and roast, turning them from time to time, until softened slightly and blackened in spots, about 6 minutes. Turn off the heat, remove the vegetables from the skillet, and set aside to cool at room temperature. Once they are cool enough to handle, peel the garlic cloves and discard the skins. Remove and discard the stems of the chiles.

Place the roasted tomatillos, ground spices, garlic, onion, and chiles in a blender and puree on high speed until completely smooth, working in batches if necessary. If needed, add 1 tablespoon water to help the vegetables pass through the blades of the blender. Set up a medium-mesh sieve over a bowl and pass the puree through the strainer. Set aside.

Rinse out the blender jar, add the broth and the masa, and puree on high speed until completely smooth. Set up a medium-mesh sieve over a second bowl and pass the puree through the strainer. Set aside.

Rinse out the blender jar again, and add the cilantro, parsley, epazote, and hoja santa leaves, along with 2 cups of water. Puree on high speed until completely smooth. Set up a medium-mesh sieve over a third bowl and pass the puree through the strainer. Set aside.

Add the lard to a tall, 6-quart nonreactive stockpot and heat over medium heat until smoking. Pour in the tomatillo-chile puree all at once; the puree will sputter. Lower the heat to a simmer as you stir the mixture with a wooden spoon. Continue stirring until the puree reaches a porridge-like consistency, about 7 minutes.

Add the masa-broth mixture to the stockpot and stir to combine. Simmer for 6 minutes, or until the mixture thickens and deepens slightly in color, then add the herb puree and the salt and sugar. Let the mixture return to a simmer, then remove from the heat. The finished mole should be the consistency of a cream soup and have a bright green color. Let the mole cool to room temperature. Transfer to a container and refrigerate until ready to use. The mole will keep for up to 3 days.

PORK RIND TACOS WITH MOLE VERDE (PAGE 136)

NUT- AND SEED-BASED
SALSAS AND MOLES

Here's where shit gets real. Nuts and seeds have been added to Mexican food for centuries to thicken sauces and fill hungry bellies. These ingredients also provide richness and a depth of flavor that can be endlessly stretched and built upon. Time and patience are as fundamental to these salsas as the ingredients themselves, which is to say that if you're tempted to try an intense, velvety Mole Poblano—one of the most elaborate dishes in all of gastronomy—you'll want to experiment with some of the other recipes in this section first. They're arranged in order of complexity, beginning with a relatively simple Salsa Macha (opposite), which is basically toasted nuts and seeds ground with spices.

When you get into the more involved preparations here, you really start to see how Americans are still limited in the way we understand and characterize certain Mexican foods. The word *salsa* translates simply as "sauce." (In fact, so does the word *mole*—that's the pre-Hispanic word for "sauce," as in guaca*mole* or *Mole* Poblano.) In the States, though, we have a more specific definition of salsa: a garnish, something to dip a chip into, and not the central component of a dish. But then, think of Italian bolognese or Indian curry. Sauce isn't always ornamental; sauce can be the point. That's where your head should be when you're making a mole or a pumpkin seed pipián.

SALSA MACHA

I was in the eastern Mexican state of Veracruz when I first encountered this strange and magnificent infused-oil salsa. It tastes like the offspring of Szechuan chile oil and Frank's RedHot, which is to say it is delicious to the point of being narcotic. It works well on just about anything and it lasts for a long time in your refrigerator, thanks to the vinegar content. Like so many Mexican recipes, there are countless versions of this salsa, fortified with different nuts and seeds and spiked with various chiles. I love the way the tiny, hot árbols complement the natural richness of the peanuts and sesame seeds, but work with what you've got in your pantry—piquín chiles and almonds make a great macha, too.

MAKES ABOUT 1½ CUPS

12 árbol chiles

½ cup vegetable oil

½ cup raw, shelled, unsalted peanuts

2 tablespoons hulled sesame seeds

3 garlic cloves, peeled

1 canned chipotle chile

1 cup cider vinegar

1 tablespoon kosher salt

1 tablespoon honey

Remove the stems from the árbol chiles and gently roll the chiles between your fingers to remove the seeds. Discard the seeds.

Set a 2-quart nonreactive saucepan over medium heat and add the vegetable oil, peanuts, sesame seeds, and garlic cloves. Cook, stirring, until the peanuts and sesame seeds are golden and the garlic cloves begin to brown, about 5 minutes.

Remove the saucepan from the heat. Add the árbol and chipotle chiles to the saucepan and set aside to steep for 10 minutes.

Place the mixture in a blender along with the vinegar, salt, and honey and puree on high speed until completely smooth. Set up a medium-mesh sieve over a bowl and pass the puree through the strainer. Let cool to room temperature. Transfer to a container and refrigerate until ready to use. The salsa will keep for up to 1 month.

SIKIL PAK

Mexican cuisine is a rich example of indigenous fusion: Spanish, Moorish, even Lebanese influences are deeply interwoven with the country's native pantry. So to understand the pre-Hispanic flavors of Mexico, you have to look back to an ancient recipe like sikil pak. The secrets of this addictive Yucatecan dip are hidden in its Mayan name: Sikil (pumpkin seeds) and p'ak (tomatoes) are roasted and ground together, along with the region's most prevalent chile, the habanero. This stuff is like alpha-hummus, packed with protein and engineered for compulsive snacking. I use half a habanero to get the spice just right, but you can add more or less of the chile depending on your heat preference.

MAKES ABOUT 2¾ CUPS

1 plum tomato

One 2-inch stick of canela (Mexican cinnamon)

2 cups raw, hulled, unsalted pepitas (pumpkin seeds)

1 habanero chile

3 garlic cloves, skins on

½ medium white onion, cut into ¼-inch-thick slices

1 sour orange (substitute a lime if you can't find this fruit)

1 teaspoon kosher salt

60 cilantro leaves (from about 15 sprigs)

Preheat the broiler. Roast the tomato on a baking sheet under the broiler until blackened in spots, about 7 minutes. Turn it over and continue to blacken, another 7 minutes. Remove from the broiler and set aside to cool at room temperature. Once it is cool enough to handle, peel the tomato and discard the skin.

Set a 12-inch cast-iron skillet over medium heat for 5 minutes. Add the canela and toast, shaking the pan, until fragrant, about 15 seconds. Remove from the heat, transfer to a spice grinder, and grind to a fine powder.

Reheat the skillet over medium heat. Toast the pepitas until they puff up and turn brown, shaking the pan constantly to prevent them from burning. Remove from the heat and transfer to the bowl of a food processor. Grind the pepitas until a powder forms and begins to stick to the sides of the bowl.

Reheat the skillet, then roast the habanero, garlic cloves, and onion slices, turning them from time to time, until softened slightly and blackened in spots, about 6 minutes. Turn off the heat, remove the vegetables from the skillet, and set aside to cool at room temperature. Once they are cool enough to handle, peel the garlic cloves and discard the skins.

Add the roasted tomato, garlic, onion, and half of the habanero to the bowl of the food processor with the ground pepitas. Cut the sour orange in half and squeeze over a medium-mesh strainer directly into the bowl. Add the ground canela, salt, and cilantro leaves, along with ¾ cup water; pulse to a coarse puree. Transfer to a container and refrigerate until ready to use. The sikil pak will keep for up to 3 days.

PINE NUT SALSA

The inspiration for this salsa is an Oaxacan dish known as almendrado—typically, meat stewed in a sauce of almonds, raisins, capers, olives, and spices. The idea of transforming a long-simmered braise into something as nimble and versatile as a salsa was compelling. To get there, we swapped the almonds for pine nuts (their oil content makes for a smoother puree), and turned up the clove and cinnamon to push the winter-spice warmth that almendrado is known for.

MAKES ABOUT 2 CUPS

2 plum tomatoes

½ teaspoon dried Mexican oregano

1 whole clove

One 2-inch stick of canela (Mexican cinnamon)

2 garlic cloves, skins on

¼ cup plus ½ tablespoon lard or vegetable oil

½ medium white onion, thinly sliced

½ cup pine nuts

2 tablespoons golden raisins

10 manzanilla olives, pitted

1 teaspoon kosher salt

3 tablespoons cider vinegar

1 tablespoon honey

Preheat the broiler. Roast the tomatoes on a baking sheet under the broiler until blackened in spots, about 7 minutes. Turn them over and continue to blacken, another 7 minutes. Remove from the broiler and set aside to cool at room temperature. Once they are cool enough to handle, peel the tomatoes, discard the skins, and set aside.

Set a 12-inch cast-iron skillet over medium heat for 5 minutes. Add the oregano, clove, and canela and toast, shaking the pan, until fragrant, about 15 seconds. Remove from the heat, transfer to a spice grinder, and grind to a fine powder.

Reheat the skillet over medium heat. Add the garlic cloves and roast, turning them from time to time, until softened slightly and blackened in spots, about 6 minutes. Turn off the heat, remove garlic from the skillet, and set aside to cool at room temperature. Once they are cool enough to handle, peel the garlic cloves and discard the skins.

Place a 4-quart nonreactive saucepan over medium heat. Add ½ tablespoon of the lard and heat until shimmering. Add the onion and sweat until translucent. Remove from the heat and set aside.

Add the remaining ¼ cup lard to the skillet and heat over medium heat until shimmering. Set up a plate lined with paper towels. Fry the pine nuts until golden brown, about 1 minute. Remove the pine nuts with a slotted spoon and transfer to the prepared plate to drain.

In the same skillet, fry the golden raisins until puffed, about 30 seconds, and transfer to the plate to drain with the pine nuts. Remove the pan from the heat.

Place the roasted tomatoes, ground spices, garlic, onion, pine nuts, and raisins in a blender. Add the olives, salt, vinegar, and honey and puree until coarse. Transfer to a container and refrigerate until ready to use. The salsa will keep for up to 3 days.

PIPIÁN

Commonly served like a stew with meat or poultry, pipián is a thick sauce that derives its spicy, nutty flavor from seeds and chiles. It can be found all over Mexico in red and green varieties, but this specific version is Yucatecan—distinct for its use of slightly bitter achiote along with the pumpkin and sesame seeds, smoky chipotle, and searing árbols. I finish this recipe with shrimp broth to help marry its flavors with the Grilled Shrimp Tacos (page 177), but you can certainly use whatever broth you have on hand. If you want to try pipián in a more traditional context, just add your raw protein to a pot of the simmering sauce, braise until tender, and serve with rice or tortillas.

MAKES ABOUT 2¼ CUPS

1 plum tomato

6 árbol chiles

¼ teaspoon dried Mexican oregano

2 allspice berries

2 whole cloves

1 pinch cumin seeds

3 garlic cloves, skins on

¼ medium white onion, cut into ¼-inch-thick slices

1½ tablespoons hulled sesame seeds

1½ tablespoons achiote seeds

6 tablespoons lard or vegetable oil

1 cup raw, hulled, unsalted pepitas (pumpkin seeds)

1 canned chipotle chile

1 cup Shrimp Broth (page 231) or water

1½ tablespoons kosher salt

1 tablespoon sugar

1 tablespoon cider vinegar

Preheat the broiler. Roast the tomato on a baking sheet under the broiler until blackened in spots, about 7 minutes. Turn it over and continue to blacken, another 7 minutes. Remove from the broiler and set aside to cool at room temperature. Once it is cool enough to handle, peel the tomato, discard the skin, and set aside on a plate.

Remove the stems from the árbol chiles and gently roll the chiles between your fingers to remove the seeds. Discard the seeds.

Set a 12-inch cast-iron skillet over medium heat for 5 minutes. Add the oregano, allspice berries, cloves, and cumin seeds; toast, shaking the pan, until fragrant, about 15 seconds. Remove from the heat, transfer to a spice grinder, and grind to a fine powder. Transfer to a bowl.

Reheat the skillet over medium heat. Add the garlic cloves and onion slices and roast, turning them from time to time, until softened slightly and blackened in spots, about 6 minutes. Remove the vegetables from the skillet and set aside to cool at room temperature. Once they are cool enough to handle, peel the garlic cloves and discard the skins. Transfer to the plate with the roasted tomato.

In the skillet, toast the sesame seeds until golden brown, shaking the pan frequently to prevent them from burning, about 15 seconds. Remove from the heat and transfer to the bowl with the ground spices. Next, toast the achiote seeds, shaking the pan until fragrant, about 15 seconds. Remove from the heat and add to the bowl with the spices and sesame seeds.

recipe continues

Add 4 tablespoons lard to the skillet and heat until shimmering. Line a plate with paper towels. Fry the árbol chiles for 30 seconds, until they deepen in color and blister slightly, then use a slotted spoon to transfer them to the prepared plate to drain. Place the chiles in a large bowl and cover with hot tap water, putting a heavy plate on the chiles to keep them submerged. Set aside to soak for 30 minutes.

Set up a second plate lined with paper towels. Reheat the skillet over medium heat and fry the pepitas until puffed and golden, about 45 seconds. Remove the seeds with a slotted spoon and transfer to the prepared plate to drain. Set aside.

By now, you should have four separate preparations: (1) the ground spice and seed mixture; (2) the roasted tomato, garlic, and onion; (3) the soaking árbol chiles; (4) the fried pepitas.

Drain the árbol chiles and place in a blender along with the ground spice and seed mixture; the roasted tomato, garlic, and onion; the fried pepitas; and the chipotle chile and 2 cups fresh water. Puree on high speed until completely smooth, working in batches if necessary. Set up a medium-mesh sieve over a bowl and pass the puree through the strainer. Set aside.

Add the remaining 2 tablespoons lard to a tall, 6-quart nonreactive stockpot and heat over medium heat until smoking. Pour in the puree all at once; the puree will sputter. Lower the heat to a simmer as you stir the mixture with a wooden spoon. Continue stirring as you cook the puree down to a thick paste, about 15 minutes. Be careful as you stir; the puree will continue to sputter as it reduces.

Add the broth and bring to a simmer. Season with the salt, sugar, and vinegar and cook for another 15 minutes, until the consistency resembles a cream soup. Remove from the heat and let cool to room temperature. Transfer to a container and refrigerate until ready to use. The pipián will keep for a week, or you can freeze it for up to 1 month.

ARGAN OIL MOLE

Is mole a recipe, or is it a technique? I've engaged in heated debates with Mexican chefs about this topic, and I know where I stand. There's no "true" recipe for a mole, and swapping in different nuts, seeds, spices, chiles, and fruits can transform its character. I'd argue that what defines a mole isn't the ingredients themselves but how they are manipulated.

Thinking of mole as a compass rather than a road map opens up a whole world of creative thinking. Raisins are common in Mole Poblano recipes, so for this North African–inspired variation, we reach for the concentrated sweetness of dried apricots and prunes instead. And rather than finish the sauce with rich chocolate, we call for argan oil. Derived from the kernels within the nuts of the Moroccan argan tree, this bright, nutty liquid offers one of the most exotic flavors I've come across—like almonds bathed in orange flower water. It is also a common cosmetic additive, so make sure you buy a bottle that's suitable for your pantry—you can find that at retailers like Kalustyan's (see Resources).

MAKES ABOUT 4 CUPS

2 plum tomatoes

12 guajillo chiles

2 chipotle morita chiles

One 3-inch stick of canela (Mexican cinnamon)

3 pieces of star anise

6 whole cloves

1 teaspoon coriander seeds

6 tablespoons hulled sesame seeds

6 garlic cloves, skins on

½ medium white onion, cut into ¼-inch-thick slices

1 cup lard or vegetable oil

½ cup whole almonds, blanched

½ cup whole hazelnuts, blanched

4 dried apricots

4 prunes

2 cups Chicken Broth (page 230) or water

1 cup argan oil

2 tablespoons honey

2 tablespoons kosher salt

Preheat the broiler. Roast the tomatoes on a baking sheet under the broiler until blackened in spots, about 7 minutes. Turn them over and continue to blacken, another 7 minutes. Remove from the broiler and set aside to cool at room temperature. Once they are cool enough to handle, peel the tomatoes and discard the skins. Transfer to a plate.

Remove the stems from the guajillo and chipotle chiles and tear the chiles open. Shake out and discard the seeds. Remove and discard the veins. Tear the chiles into small pieces.

Set a 12-inch cast-iron skillet over medium heat for 5 minutes. Add the canela, star anise, cloves, and coriander seeds; toast, shaking the pan, until fragrant, 15 seconds. Remove from the heat, transfer to a spice grinder, and grind to a fine powder. Transfer to a bowl.

Reheat the skillet over medium heat. Toast the sesame seeds until golden brown, shaking the pan frequently to prevent them from burning, about 45 seconds. Remove from the heat and transfer to the bowl with the ground spices.

Reheat the skillet. Roast the garlic cloves and onion slices in the skillet, turning them from time to time, until softened slightly and blackened in spots, about 6 minutes. Remove the vegetables from the skillet and set aside to cool at room temperature. Once they are cool enough to handle, peel the garlic cloves and discard the skins. Transfer to the plate with the roasted tomatoes.

recipe continues

Add the lard to the skillet and heat until shimmering. Set up a plate lined with paper towels. Working in batches, fry the chile pieces for about 30 seconds, until they blister and deepen in color. Use a slotted spoon to transfer the chiles to the prepared plate to drain. Place the drained chiles in a large bowl and cover with 6 cups hot tap water, putting a heavy plate on the chiles to keep them submerged. Set aside to soak for 30 minutes.

Set up a second plate lined with paper towels. Fry the almonds in the lard until dark brown, about 2 minutes. Remove the almonds with a slotted spoon and transfer to the second plate to drain.

Fry the hazelnuts until golden brown, about 1 minute, then transfer to drain along with the almonds. Next, fry the dried apricots and prunes until the apricots turn dark brown, about 30 seconds, then transfer to the plate to drain. Pour the lard from the skillet into a heatproof bowl and reserve 2 tablespoons.

By now, you should have four separate preparations: (1) the ground spices and sesame seeds; (2) the roasted tomatoes, garlic, and onion; (3) the soaking chiles; (4) the fried nuts and fruit.

Drain the chiles, reserving 4 cups of the soaking liquid. Place the chiles in a blender along with the reserved liquid. Puree the chiles on high speed until completely smooth, working in batches if necessary. Place a medium-mesh sieve over a bowl and pass the puree through the strainer. Set the chile puree aside.

Rinse out the blender jar and add the ground spices and sesame seeds along with the roasted tomatoes, garlic, and onion and the fried nuts and fruit. Add 4 cups water to the jar and puree on high speed until completely smooth, working in batches if necessary. Set up a medium-mesh sieve over a second bowl and pass the puree through the strainer. Set aside.

Add the 2 tablespoons of reserved lard to a tall, 6-quart nonreactive stockpot and heat over medium heat until smoking. Pour in the chile puree all at once; the puree will sputter. Lower the heat to a simmer as you stir the mixture with a wooden spoon. Continue stirring as you cook the puree down to a thick paste, about 30 minutes. Be careful as you stir; the puree will continue to sputter as it reduces.

Add the spice/tomato/nut puree to the pot and stir to combine. Continue cooking until reduced to a thick paste again, about 30 minutes.

Add the broth to the mole and let it come to a simmer. Add the argan oil and whisk until completely combined. Season the mole with the honey and salt, and cook for another 15 minutes, until the consistency resembles a cream soup. Remove from the heat and let cool to room temperature. Transfer to a container and refrigerate until ready to use. The mole will keep for a week, or you can freeze it for up to 1 month.

BURNT CHILES FOR CHILMOLE

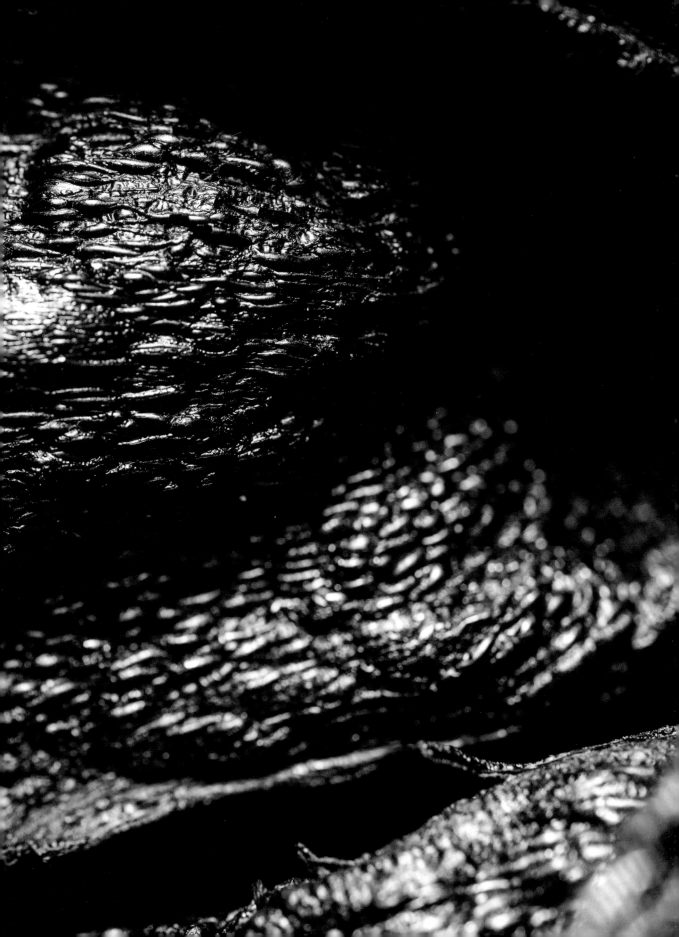

MOLE POBLANO

Like skydiving or driving a really expensive car, cooking a Mole Poblano is the sort of thing you ought to do at least once in your lifetime.
It's bucket-list cooking at its finest: inconvenient as hell to make, with
each ingredient requiring its own, unique conditioning. Mole Poblano
is culinary masonry—mighty and architectural, built brick by brick by
laborious brick. It's considered a serious undertaking even in Mexico.
Keep your eyes peeled at the markets and you'll spot cheater mole pastes,
arranged on tables in dense, dark anthills for time-strapped cooks to
take home.

So why make it at all? Well, for starters, it's just a uniquely delicious
thing: complex, layered, and symphonic, with dried chiles giving way
to warm spices, nuts, and raisiny sweetness. But there are also some Mr.
Miyagi lessons in the doing: toast spices, baptize nuts and chiles in hot
lard, concentrate a puree, thin it out with flavor-packed stock, and mount
the sauce with rich chocolate. Wax on, wax off, and you get it—the
flavors you develop and the motions you go through to prepare Mole
Poblano are emblematic of everything Mexican cuisine has to offer. All
the depth and the diligence and the history and the ingenuity. Welcome
to the deep end, my friend.

Most of the salsas in this chapter match up with a taco recipe in the
next chapter, but Mole Poblano stands alone. It's such an intensive thing
to make that I didn't want to reduce it to a garnish. To really showcase
the mole, try serving it with Chicken Tortillas (page 55). The meat in
the tortilla is a nod to the way mole is commonly served in Mexico, with
poultry simply poached in the sauce.

MAKES ABOUT 4 CUPS

2 plum tomatoes

1 medium tomatillo, husked, rinsed,
  and patted dry

6 ancho chiles

2 pasilla chiles

6 guajillo chiles

One 2-inch stick of canela (Mexican
  cinnamon)

½ teaspoon anise seeds

½ teaspoon black peppercorns

2 whole cloves

½ teaspoon coriander seeds

½ teaspoon dried thyme

½ teaspoon dried Mexican oregano

3 tablespoons hulled sesame seeds

6 garlic cloves, skins on

½ medium white onion, cut into
  ¼-inch-thick slices

1 cup lard or vegetable oil

2 tablespoons raw, hulled, unsalted
  pepitas (pumpkin seeds)

¼ cup whole almonds, blanched

¼ cup raw, shelled, unsalted
  peanuts

¼ cup raisins

1 corn tortilla

1 slice white bread

2 cups Chicken Broth (page 230)
  or water

1½ ounces Mexican chocolate,
  such as Abuelita

2 tablespoons sugar

2 tablespoons kosher salt

Preheat the broiler. Roast the tomatoes and tomatillo on a baking sheet under the broiler until blackened in spots, about 7 minutes. Turn them over and continue to blacken, another 7 minutes. Remove from the broiler and set aside to cool at room temperature. Once they are cool enough to handle, peel the tomatoes, discard the skins, and set aside with the roasted tomatillo.

Remove the stems from the ancho, pasilla, and guajillo chiles and tear the chiles open. Shake out the seeds over a bowl and reserve 1 tablespoon of them, discarding the rest. Remove and discard the veins. Tear the chiles into small pieces.

Set a 12-inch cast-iron skillet over medium heat for 5 minutes. Toast the reserved 1 tablespoon of chile seeds until they turn dark golden brown, 15 to 20 seconds. Remove from the heat and transfer the seeds to a bowl.

In the same skillet, combine the canela, anise seeds, peppercorns, cloves, coriander seeds, thyme, and oregano. Toast, shaking the pan, until fragrant, about 15 seconds. Remove from the heat, transfer to a spice grinder, and grind to a fine powder. Transfer to the bowl with the toasted chile seeds.

Reheat the skillet over medium heat. Toast the sesame seeds until dark golden brown, shaking the

pan constantly to prevent them from burning, about 15 seconds. Remove from the heat and transfer to the bowl. Set aside.

Place the garlic cloves and onion slices in the skillet and roast, turning them occasionally, until softened slightly and blackened in spots, about 6 minutes. Remove the vegetables from the skillet and set aside to cool at room temperature. Once they are cool enough to handle, peel the garlic cloves and discard the skins. Set aside with the tomatillo and tomatoes.

Add the lard to the skillet, still over medium heat, and heat until shimmering. Line a plate with paper towels. Working in batches, fry the chile pieces for about 30 seconds, until they blister and deepen in color. Use a slotted spoon to transfer the chiles to the prepared plate to drain. Place the drained chiles in a large bowl and cover with 6 cups hot tap water, putting a heavy plate on the chiles to keep them submerged. Set aside to soak for 30 minutes.

Line a second plate with paper towels. Fry the pumpkin seeds in the lard until puffed and golden, about 45 seconds. Remove the seeds with a slotted spoon and transfer to the second prepared plate to drain.

Next, fry the almonds until dark brown, about 2 minutes, then remove to drain along with the pumpkin seeds. Fry the peanuts

until they are golden brown, about 1 minute, and transfer to drain. Fry the raisins until they puff up, about 30 seconds, and transfer to drain. Fry the corn tortilla until dark golden brown, carefully flipping it as needed with tongs, about 2 minutes. Transfer to the plate to drain. Finally, fry the slice of bread until golden brown, flipping it as needed, about 1 minute. Remove from the lard and transfer to drain. Pour the lard from the skillet into a heatproof bowl and reserve 2 tablespoons.

By now, you should have four separate preparations: (1) the toasted chile seeds, sesame seeds, and ground herbs and spices; (2) the soaking chiles; (3) the roasted tomatillo, tomatoes, garlic, and onion; (4) the fried seeds, nuts, tortilla, and bread.

Drain the chiles, reserving 4 cups of the soaking liquid. Place the chiles in a blender along with the reserved liquid. Puree the chiles on high speed until completely smooth, working in batches if necessary. Place a medium-mesh sieve over a large bowl and pass the puree through the strainer. Set the chile puree aside.

Rinse out the blender jar and add the toasted chile seeds, sesame seeds, and ground herbs and spices, along with the roasted tomatillo, tomatoes, garlic, and onion, and add the fried seeds, nuts, tortilla, and bread. Add

recipe continues

4 cups water to the jar and puree on high speed until completely smooth. Place a medium-mesh sieve over a clean bowl and pass the puree through the strainer. Set the puree aside.

Add the 2 tablespoons reserved lard to a tall, 6-quart nonreactive stockpot and heat over medium heat until smoking. Pour in the chile puree all at once; the puree will sputter. Lower the heat to a simmer as you stir the mixture with a wooden spoon. Continue stirring as you cook the puree down to a thick, dark paste, about 45 minutes. Be careful as you stir; the puree will continue to sputter as it reduces.

Add the tomato-spice-nut puree and stir to combine. Continue cooking until reduced to a thick, dark paste again, about 1 hour.

Add the broth to the mole and let it come to a simmer. Stir in the chocolate to melt it into the mole. Season the mole with the sugar and salt, and continue to simmer for another 15 minutes, until the consistency resembles a cream soup. Remove from the heat and let cool to room temperature. Transfer to a container and refrigerate until ready to use. The mole will keep for a week, or you can freeze it for up to 1 month.

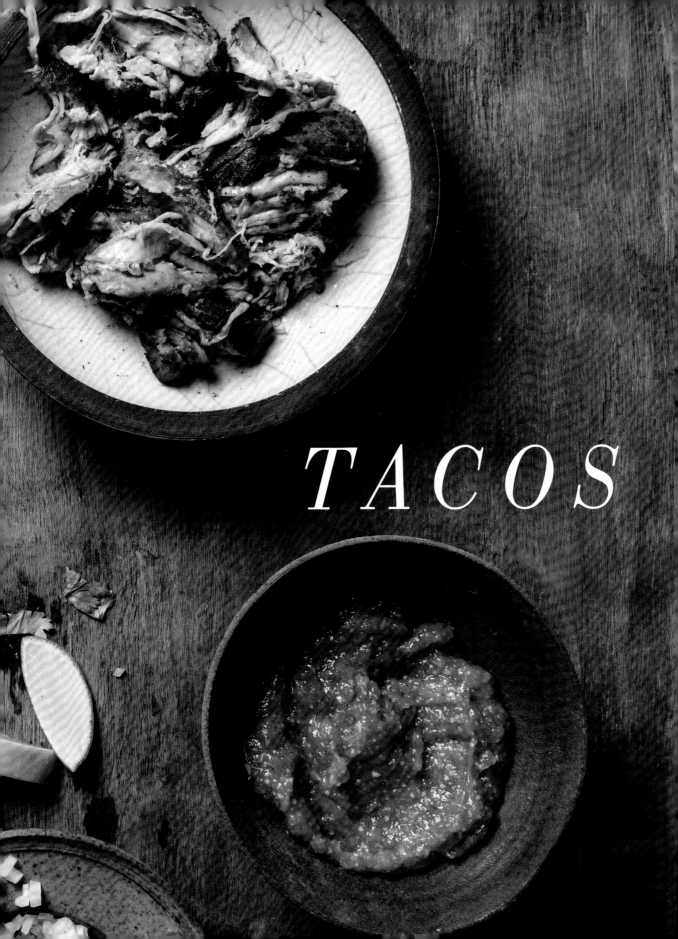

TACOS

All that kneading of masa and seeding of chiles makes fantastic sense when you taste what fresh tortillas and homemade salsas can do for a taco. Here's where it all comes together.

There are classic fillings in this book, like Oaxacan barbacoa perfumed with banana leaves. But there are also tacos that regard tradition as a starting point, and still others that diverge from it entirely, using my own background as inspiration instead. You wouldn't see a pastrami taco in Mexico, but in New York City where I live and cook, that's a leap that makes sense to me. I'm a New England kid with modernist pastry credentials, so there are fried oysters, crab cakes, and foamy emulsions, too. I don't apologize for continuing to ask questions of an ancient cuisine—or for letting it evolve in my hands. But when I explore canonical foods, I also don't want to sand away their otherness with the goal of making them familiar. Interesting stuff happens when respect for tradition collides with fresh ideas—that's the sweet spot I reach for here.

Most of these taco recipes are paired with salsas that appear in this book. These, and anything else you should have ready to go before making the tacos, are marked as "advanced preparation." I highly recommend you take the opportunity to work ahead and save the last-minute cooking for the actual tortillas. Because I put so much emphasis on the importance of making your own tortillas, I've given careful thought to placement of that step in each of these taco recipes. The idea is to make the salsas, take the fillings as far as possible, then make the tortillas, so that you can serve them at their peak, still hot from the griddle.

CHICKEN TACOS
WITH KALE AND SALSA VERDE

The flavors in this taco are some of the first I fell in love with in Mexican cooking. This is one of the most straightforward recipes in the book, but it's also a tidy summary of the Mexican larder: the spark of cilantro, tomatillo, and chile in the salsa; the mild dairy richness of crema and queso fresco; tangy lime juice; and simple roasted meat. This taco is a staple on the menu at Empellón Taqueria, and it's an excellent entry point for a home cook.

MAKES 12 TACOS

ADVANCE PREPARATION

1 recipe Raw Salsa Verde (page 78)

Crema Mexicana (page 233), for serving

FOR THE FILLING

6 bone-in, skin-on chicken thighs (about 1½ pounds)

2 tablespoons lard or vegetable oil

Kosher salt, as needed

1 bunch of kale, any variety, stemmed and shredded (about 2½ cups)

TO ASSEMBLE THE TACOS

1 cup queso fresco, crumbled

½ medium white onion, minced

60 cilantro leaves (from about 15 sprigs), roughly chopped

2 limes, each cut into 6 wedges

1 recipe Corn or Flour Tortillas (page 35 or 41)

MAKE THE FILLING: Preheat the oven to 350°F. Rub the chicken thighs with the lard and season liberally with salt. Transfer the chicken thighs to a baking sheet skin side up and roast for 45 minutes, or until golden and cooked through. Remove from the oven and let rest for 30 minutes.

Transfer the chicken to a cutting board and peel away the skin. Finely chop the skin and transfer to a bowl. Pick the chicken meat from the bones and cut into medium chunks. Transfer to the bowl with the chopped skin along with any juices that have accumulated on the cutting board.

Set a 4-quart saucepan over medium heat and add the Raw Salsa Verde. Bring to a simmer and add the kale. Cook until the greens have wilted, about 5 minutes. Add the chopped chicken to the saucepan and heat through. Taste and adjust the seasoning with salt, then set aside in a warm place.

Make one batch of tortillas and hold them warm.

ASSEMBLE THE TACOS: Lay out the warm tortillas on plates. Evenly distribute the chicken mixture among the tortillas and top with the Crema Mexicana, the queso fresco, minced onion, and chopped cilantro. Squeeze a couple of the lime wedges over the tacos and serve the rest on the side.

CHICKEN TACOS
WITH CHILMOLE

Although the ingredients are fairly simple—just spices, garlic, vinegar, and a metric ton of árbols and anchos—making the burnt chile paste known as chilmole is a serious task. Incinerating chiles will hijack your kitchen, and you'll be coughing through airborne capsaicin as you wave smoke away from your fire alarm. You'll forget all that trouble when you taste the stuff, of course, with its muted heat and toasty notes of coffee, caramel, and ash. But if you're going to take on chilmole, whatever you serve it with ought to be simple enough to let the flavors shine through. This taco is really just a showcase for the chilmole: roasted chicken thighs, some simple aromatics, and a squirt of rich crema to help carry the flavor.

MAKES 12 TACOS

ADVANCE PREPARATION

¼ cup Chilmole (page 225)

Crema Mexicana (page 233), for serving

FOR THE FILLING

8 bone-in, skin-on chicken thighs (about 2 pounds)

3 tablespoons lard or vegetable oil

Kosher salt, as needed

½ medium white onion, minced

2 jalapeño chiles, roughly chopped

4 plum tomatoes, diced

TO ASSEMBLE THE TACOS

½ medium white onion, minced

60 cilantro leaves (from about 15 sprigs), roughly chopped

2 limes, each cut into 6 wedges

1 recipe Corn or Flour Tortillas (page 35 or 41)

MAKE THE FILLING: Preheat the oven to 350°F. Rub the chicken thighs with 2 tablespoons of the lard and season liberally with salt. Transfer the chicken to a baking sheet, skin side up, and roast the chicken thighs for 45 minutes, or until golden and cooked through. Remove from the oven and let rest for 30 minutes.

Transfer the chicken thighs to a cutting board. Peel away and discard the skin. Pick the chicken meat from the bones and cut into medium chunks. Transfer to a bowl.

Set a 4-quart saucepan over medium heat and add the remaining 1 tablespoon lard. Once the fat is shimmering, add the onion and jalapeños and season with salt. Cook until the onion is translucent. Add the tomatoes to the saucepan and cook until their liquid has mostly evaporated, about 5 minutes. Add the Chilmole and cook for another 2 minutes. Taste and adjust the seasoning with salt.

Transfer the chicken to the saucepan and stir to coat evenly. Set aside in a warm place.

Make one batch of tortillas and hold them warm.

ASSEMBLE THE TACOS: Lay out the warm tortillas on serving plates. Evenly distribute the chicken mixture among the tortillas and top with a drizzle of Crema Mexicana, minced onion, and chopped cilantro. Squeeze a couple of the lime wedges over the tacos and serve the rest on the side.

CHICKEN WING TACOS
WITH SALSA MACHA

The first time I tasted vinegary, wicked-hot salsa macha, it made me think instantly of Frank's RedHot sauce and, by extension, of buffalo wings. This taco brings that affinity full circle, with confit chicken wings and a garnish of crunchy celery and blue cheese. If I were the sort of man who didn't vehemently hate football, I'd probably eat a tray of these tacos with a bowl of chicharrones while watching the game with my bros. This taco is delicious anytime, though. Even if you are not a bro.

MAKES 12 TACOS

ADVANCE PREPARATION

1 recipe Salsa Macha (page 89)

FOR THE FILLING

24 chicken wings (about 4½ pounds)

Kosher salt, as needed

12 garlic cloves, peeled

6 cups lard, melted

TO ASSEMBLE THE TACOS

1 celery heart, split in half lengthwise

1 cup roasted, salted peanuts, roughly chopped

6 ounces blue cheese, such as Cabrales or Gorgonzola dolce, crumbled (about ¾ cup)

2 limes, each cut into 6 wedges

1 recipe Corn or Flour Tortillas (page 35 or 41)

MAKE THE FILLING: Preheat the oven to 350°F. Remove the tips and drumsticks from the chicken wings and reserve for another use. Season the remaining chicken wings liberally with salt and nestle them in a 5½-quart Dutch oven with the garlic cloves. Pour the melted lard over the wings to cover and top with a lid. Place in the oven and cook for 90 minutes, or until fork-tender.

Remove the Dutch oven from the oven and let rest covered and undisturbed for 1 hour at room temperature. With a slotted spoon, transfer the chicken wings to a baking sheet and gently remove the bones, keeping the wing pieces as intact as possible. Arrange the wings skin side up and refrigerate for at least 1 hour, or overnight.

Preheat the broiler. Brush the chicken wings with some of the Salsa Macha and place under the broiler until they sizzle and the salsa bakes into them, about 3 minutes. Set aside in a warm place.

Make one batch of tortillas and hold them warm.

ASSEMBLE THE TACOS: Lay out the warm tortillas on serving plates. Place 2 chicken wings on each tortilla and drizzle with some of the remaining Salsa Macha. Top with the celery, peanuts, and blue cheese. Squeeze a couple of the lime wedges over the tacos and serve the rest on the side.

MY BEEF WITH
BEEF

Chat with enough Mexican chefs about the American perception of their food, and you'll find that one particular object of scorn sums it up: the gringo ground beef taco. You know the one. The yellow shell is folded into a crispy, crunchy parabola. It's stuffed with pebbly orange meat, iceberg lettuce, and drifts of cheddar cheese. There are probably a lot of reasons why Mexican chefs don't see themselves in this portrait we've drawn of their cuisine. But there's one thing about the taco that must seem particularly off: It's made with beef.

Of the holy trinity of American proteins—beef, chicken, and pork—beef is the least consumed in Mexico. And yet here in the United States, our revisionist version of that country's cuisine casts it in a starring role. That's not entirely surprising, though. After all, we are a nation of steak lovers. We exalt the tender, marbled muscles that reside in the center of the beast. We pay up for these cuts and pass the rest of them through a meat grinder. That's good news, too, because we eat an awful lot of burgers around these parts.

In this context of bovine bloodlust it makes some sense that beef came along for the ride, as Mexican cuisine was made to assimilate to American tastes. Sizzling platters of skirt steak fajitas are the prestige order at every fast-casual nightmare. Old El Paso and their ilk have made an industry of peddling products to spice up your hamburger at home. The great, creative minds of our time now work for Taco Bell, devising ever-bigger, ever-badder ways to dress up and sell ground beef for under two bucks.

And down in Mexico, everyone is just shaking their heads. Ground beef is particularly uncommon there, and it's difficult to find recipes that call for it in Mexican cookbooks. The closest thing I've landed on is picadillo (see page 118), and even then, many of the recipes favor shredded pork. There is a cattle industry in Mexico, and you can certainly buy beef there, although you might not recognize it. It is often sold in massive, salted sheets called *cecina* or *tasajo* in Oaxaca. It is tough and fibrous, owing to both the cow itself (Mexican cattle are muscular enough to qualify for the Olympics) and the way it is butchered—with the grain rather than against it. This beef will never melt in your mouth, and the best thing you can do to tenderize it is to cook it hard and fast on a blazing-hot griddle and then hack it to bits with a machete. Beef cooked this way can be delicious, especially stuffed in a taco. But even still, the meat just doesn't have nearly the prevalence in Mexico that it does in the States.

This is just one example of how un-Mexican our idea of Mexican cuisine truly is. It's disturbing to think that many Americans probably don't realize how little their image of Mexican food has to do with the food actually eaten by most Mexican people. We edit foreign cultures to better suit our own tastes—that's just our way. If there were an Indian fast-food chain filing an IPO in America, I'd bet that beef would be the centerpiece of that menu too, despite the doleful mooing of many a sacred Hindu cow. We tell ourselves we know about the world, but sometimes what we know is just a myth we've invented and then fed back to ourselves, muffled with sour cream.

Out of the fifty tacos in this book, five of them include beef, and I like to think they help illustrate the line I walk as an American chef cooking Mexican food. The Skirt Steak Taco (page 115) is my best-selling taco at Empellón Taqueria, by many orders of magnitude; it's the taco that keeps the lights on, so that's in here. There's also a delicious ground beef Picadillo Taco (page 118), based on a recipe from a buddy of mine who lives in Merida. And there's a Cheeseburger Taco (page 121), too.

This may be America, but even Mexicans love a cheeseburger.

SKIRT STEAK TACOS
WITH MOJO DE AJO

This garlicky grilled steak number is as easy to make as it is to like. Give the meat a quick and angry char on the grill with thick slices of onion, then blast it with mojo de ajo—an oil dressing common in Veracruz cooking, charged with garlic, Mexican oregano, and orange. It's a steak taco, so you don't need me to tell you there's room to adjust for personal taste here. I like to serve it with Salsa Arriera (page 61)—that green-pepper flavor feels right with steak—but Salsa Habanera (page 62), and frankly any ripping hot salsa, would be delicious too.

MAKES 12 TACOS

ADVANCE PREPARATION

1 recipe Mojo de Ajo (page 224)

Salsa Arriera (page 61), for serving

FOR THE FILLING

Vegetable oil, for the grill

1 outside skirt steak, peeled and trimmed (about 2 pounds)

1 medium white onion, cut into 3 thick slices

Kosher salt and freshly ground black pepper, as needed

TO ASSEMBLE THE TACOS

2 limes, each cut into 6 wedges

1 recipe Corn or Flour Tortillas (page 35 or 41)

START THE FILLING: Allow the Mojo de Ajo to settle and separate the garlic pieces from the layer of oil. Reserve in separate bowls.

Preheat a grill to the hottest possible setting and brush with vegetable oil. Cut the skirt steak into three even pieces. Rub both the steak and the onion slices with about ½ cup of the reserved oil from the Mojo de Ajo and season liberally with the salt and black pepper.

Place the steaks and onion slices on the hot grill and cook for 2 minutes. Rotate 45 degrees and cook for another 2 minutes. Flip and cook for 2 minutes; rotate 45 degrees and cook for a final 2 minutes. Remove the steaks and onion from the grill, transfer to a plate, and set aside to rest in a warm place.

Make one batch of tortillas and hold them warm.

FINISH THE FILLING: On a cutting board, roughly chop the grilled onion and transfer to a bowl.

Cut each piece of grilled steak in half before thinly slicing it against the grain. Transfer the slices to the bowl with the chopped onion along with any juices that have accumulated on the cutting board. Add 3 to 4 tablespoons of the garlic from the Mojo de Ajo to the bowl and mix. Taste and adjust the seasoning with salt.

ASSEMBLE THE TACOS: Lay out the warm tortillas on serving plates. Evenly distribute the steak mixture among the tortillas and top with the Salsa Arriera. Squeeze a couple of the lime wedges over the tacos and serve the rest on the side.

SALPICÓN TACOS
WITH XNI PEC

Salpicón is an umbrella term for a shredded, chilled, or room-temperature salad found throughout Mexico. It's commonly made with crab, cazón (a small school shark), or beef—typically flank steak. But for this salpicón de res, I prefer to use brisket, simmered for hours, cooled, and pulled into ropy threads that set off the bright citrus and habanero flavors of the Xni Pec salsa. Since this taco isn't typically served warm, take special care to trim the meat after you rest it—no one wants a mouth full of cold fat.

MAKES 12 TACOS

ADVANCE PREPARATION

Xni Pec (page 71), for serving

FOR THE FILLING

One 3-pound piece of beef brisket

1 medium white onion, cut in half

3 garlic cloves, peeled

1 dried bay leaf

Kosher salt, as needed

1 tablespoon dried Mexican
    oregano

2 tablespoons cider vinegar

3 tablespoons extra-virgin olive oil

TO ASSEMBLE THE TACOS

2 limes, each cut into 6 wedges

1 recipe Corn or Flour Tortillas
    (page 35 or 41)

MAKE THE FILLING: Place a 6-quart stockpot over medium heat and add the brisket and enough water to cover by a few inches. Add the onion, garlic, and bay leaf and bring to a boil. Season with salt, lower the heat to a simmer, and cook for 3 hours, or until fork-tender. You may have to continue to add water to keep the brisket fully covered.

Set a 12-inch cast-iron skillet over medium heat for 5 minutes, then add the oregano and toast, shaking the pan until fragrant, about 15 seconds. Set aside.

When the brisket is tender, remove it from the heat and let rest undisturbed in its cooking liquid for 1 hour at room temperature. Transfer the brisket to a cutting board and scrape off and discard any excess fat. Use two forks to shred the meat.

Transfer the shredded brisket to a large bowl and add the toasted oregano, the cider vinegar, olive oil, and more salt to taste.

Make one batch of tortillas and hold them warm.

ASSEMBLE THE TACOS: Lay out the warm tortillas on serving plates. Evenly distribute the salpicón among the tortillas and top with the Xni Pec. Squeeze a couple of the lime wedges over the tacos and serve the rest on the side.

PICADILLO TACOS
WITH SALSA DE ÁRBOL

Fernand Point, a legendary French chef whose restaurant La Pyramide once thrived outside Lyon, famously said "success is the sum of a lot of small things correctly done." By that measure, failure can be lots of things done poorly. When I think about the vision of Mexican food provided by drive-thrus and fast-casual chains, that makes a lot of sense. Picadillo—a ground or shredded beef or pork hash—is a perfect illustration of what can go wrong when too many corners are cut. Flavored with onions, toasted spices, almonds, and chiles; sweetened with raisins and salted with chopped olives or capers, true picadillo is a complex and soulful thing. But replace the spices and aromatics with a powdered seasoning packet, veto the nuts and dried fruit, bury the meat in a crispy shell blasted with Dorito dust, and you have the modern American expression of picadillo: a gringo ground beef taco. This recipe, though, is a kind of cultural restitution, a ground beef taco that considers the details.

MAKES 12 TACOS

ADVANCE PREPARATION

1 recipe Red Chorizo (page 228)

Salsa de Árbol (page 65), for serving

FOR THE FILLING

½ teaspoon achiote seeds

¼ teaspoon whole cloves

¼ teaspoon allspice berries

¼ teaspoon cumin seeds

½ teaspoon black peppercorns

½ teaspoon dried Mexican oregano

⅔ cup sliced almonds

¼ cup lard or vegetable oil

¾ pound ground beef

Kosher salt, as needed

5 garlic cloves, minced

½ medium white onion, minced

2 jalapeño chiles, diced

2 plum tomatoes, diced

12 green olives, such as picholine or manzanilla, pitted and finely chopped

2 tablespoons brined capers, drained and finely chopped

2 tablespoons raisins

TO ASSEMBLE THE TACOS

2 limes, each cut into 6 wedges

1 recipe Corn or Flour Tortillas (page 35 or 41)

MAKE THE FILLING: Set a 12-inch cast-iron skillet over medium heat for 5 minutes. Add the achiote seeds, cloves, allspice berries, cumin seeds, black peppercorns, and oregano; toast, shaking the pan, until fragrant, about 15 seconds. Remove from the heat, transfer to a spice grinder, and grind to a fine powder.

Reheat the skillet over medium heat. Toast the sliced almonds until golden brown, shaking the pan frequently to prevent burning, about 30 seconds. Remove from the heat and transfer to a bowl.

Set a 12-inch sauté pan over medium heat and add 2 tablespoons of lard. Once the fat is shimmering, add the ground beef and cook, stirring, until crumbly and browned, about 10 minutes.

ACHIOTE SEEDS

Season with salt, then add the Red Chorizo and ground spices and cook, stirring, until the chorizo is crumbly, about 5 minutes. Remove the mixture from the pan and set aside.

Set the sauté pan back over medium heat and add the remaining 2 tablespoons lard. When shimmering, add the garlic, onion, and jalapeños. Season with salt and cook, stirring, until lightly browned. Add the plum tomatoes, green olives, capers, and raisins and stir over medium heat until the tomatoes have softened, about 5 minutes.

Return the beef-chorizo mixture to the sauté pan, season with salt, and cook for another 5 minutes, or until the tomato water has evaporated. Fold in the toasted almonds. Remove the pan from the heat and set aside in a warm place.

Make one batch of tortillas and hold them warm.

ASSEMBLE THE TACOS: Lay out the warm tortillas on serving plates. Evenly distribute the picadillo among the tortillas and drizzle with some of the Salsa de Árbol. Squeeze a couple of the lime wedges over the tacos and serve the rest on the side.

CHEESEBURGER TACOS

My wife, Lauren, and co-author, Jordana, discovered the cheeseburger taco together in Mexico City. We were all there for a marathon research trip to learn about al pastor—tacos filled with marinated pork shaved from a rotating spit called a *trompo*. We had 48 hours to speed through as many al pastor stands as we could reasonably manage; we had one job to do, and it didn't include any cheeseburgers. I was checking out the trompo rig at El Rey del Taco in Coyoacon when I saw Lauren and Jordana talking to the griddle cook. There was a line forming around the corner and he was passing plate after plate of the same tacos over the counter. At that time in New York, people were camping out on a SoHo sidewalk to taste a Cronut; in Mexico City, they were queuing up for cheeseburger tacos.

The women ordered one taco and we all watched as the cook prepped the griddle with lard, added a burger patty and a handful of grated cheese, and attacked the thing with a pair of metal spatulas, chopping and scraping the melty mess as if he were mixing cookie crumbles into ice cream at a Cold Stone Creamery. He swiped a flour tortilla with mayo, piled on the gooey beef, and topped it with sliced tomato and avocado. I really didn't want to like this thing. But I did. We all did.

My god, cheeseburger tacos. Cheeseburger *tacos*. The absurdity of it can take your breath away. Mexico gifted its cuisine to America, and over time we gave it a patriotic makeover, drowning its nuances in seismic waves of nacho cheese. In return, I guess, we gave them cheeseburgers. This is cultural exchange at its most mystifying. The cheeseburger taco forces some uncomfortable questions—namely, what counts as Mexican food? If the answer is simply food that's cooked by Mexicans, for Mexicans, in Mexico, using Mexican ingredients, then why is a cheeseburger taco not valid? And who is in a position to make that call? Not me, probably.

So I came back to New York, put a cheeseburger taco on the menu at Empellón Cocina, and watched it sell out every night—another cultish burger in a city that worships them. I'm not sure this taco makes a provocative statement when it is served in the United States, where there's no reason to analyze why a restaurant would offer a burger. I don't think anyone eating it at Empellón sees it as a symbol of globalization, or ponders what is gained or lost as one food culture bleeds into another. Maybe it doesn't matter. Maybe junk food is a universal golden calf and I just need to get right with the Lord. Nevertheless, you're going to love it.

Note that the filling for this taco comes together rather quickly and it must be served and eaten immediately, or else the melted cheese will seize up. For this reason, the usual taco method doesn't apply here; instead, you must make the tortillas first, and hold them warm while you prepare the cheeseburger mixture.

recipe continues

Make one batch of tortillas and hold them warm.

MAKE THE FILLING: Set a 12-inch nonstick sauté pan over medium heat and add the lard. Once the fat is shimmering, add the ground beef and cook, stirring, until crumbly and browned, about 10 minutes. Taste and adjust seasoning with salt. Add the grated cheese and stir until completely melted, about 3 minutes. Remove from the heat.

ASSEMBLE THE TACOS: Lay out the warm tortillas on serving plates. Place a tablespoon of mayonnaise on each tortilla and spread using the back of a spoon. Evenly distribute the cheeseburger filling among the tortillas and top with the tomato and avocado slices, minced onion, chopped cilantro, and a drizzle of Salsa Roja. Squeeze a couple of the lime wedges over the tacos and serve the rest on the side.

MAKES 12 TACOS

ADVANCE PREPARATION

Salsa Roja (page 68), for serving

1 recipe Corn or Flour Tortillas (page 35 or 41)

FOR THE FILLING

1 teaspoon lard or vegetable oil

1 pound ground beef

Kosher salt, as needed

1 pound Chihuahua cheese, grated

TO ASSEMBLE THE TACOS

¾ cup mayonnaise

1 plum tomato, cut into 12 slices

1 avocado, cut into 12 slices lengthwise

½ medium white onion, minced

60 cilantro leaves (from about 15 sprigs), roughly chopped

2 limes, each cut into 6 wedges

PASTRAMI TACOS
WITH MUSTARD SEED SALSA

If Mexican colonists laid down roots among the Old World delicatessens of New York City, I like to imagine that this is the bastard taco they'd cook. A multi-day brine plus a 6-hour low-and-slow roast means this dish takes advance planning. But the longer you let the pastrami cure—three days is the minimum, but a week is ideal—the better chance you have at yielding insanely tender, well-seasoned meat permeated with the flavors of brown sugar and honey. The extra time pays off in shreds of coriander-scented pastrami, cut with tart pickled cabbage and mustard seeds.

MAKES 12 TACOS

FOR THE PASTRAMI BRINE

⅔ cup kosher salt

⅔ cup packed dark brown sugar

3 teaspoons pink curing salt #1

1 tablespoon honey

FOR THE FILLING

2 pounds boneless short ribs

¼ cup black peppercorns

¼ cup coriander seeds

FOR THE PICKLED CABBAGE AND MUSTARD SEEDS

1 teaspoon cumin seeds

1 dried bay leaf

1 tablespoon black peppercorns

1 tablespoon coriander seeds

4 cups cider vinegar

½ medium white onion, thinly sliced

10 garlic cloves, peeled

2 tablespoons sugar

2 tablespoons kosher salt

½ cup mustard seeds

¼ large head of green cabbage, shredded

TO ASSEMBLE THE TACOS

½ medium white onion, minced

2 limes, each cut into 6 wedges

1 recipe Corn or Flour Tortillas (page 35 or 41)

BRINE THE PASTRAMI: In a 2-quart saucepan, combine 6 cups water with the ⅔ cup salt, brown sugar, curing salt, and honey. Bring to a simmer, then immediately remove from the heat, transfer to a bowl, and set into an ice bath to chill.

Place the short ribs in a 4-quart container with a lid. Pour the chilled brine over the meat and transfer to the refrigerator. Brine for at least 3 days and up to 1 week.

MAKE THE FILLING: Set a 12-inch cast-iron skillet over medium heat for 5 minutes. Add the peppercorns and coriander seeds and toast, shaking the pan, until fragrant, about 3 minutes. Remove from the heat, transfer to a spice grinder, and grind to a fine powder, working in batches if necessary. Set aside on a plate.

recipe continues

Preheat the oven to 300°F. Remove the short ribs from the brine and rinse under cold running water. Pat the meat dry with paper towels and transfer to the plate with the ground spices. Coat the meat completely with the spice rub. Nestle the short ribs in a 5½-quart Dutch oven. Pour in enough water so that the short ribs are half-submerged (about 2 cups) and cover tightly with a lid. Place in the oven and cook for 6 hours, or until fork-tender. Check the short ribs periodically; you may have to continue to add water to keep the level halfway up the meat.

MAKE THE PICKLED CABBAGE AND MUSTARD SEEDS: Reheat the skillet over medium heat. Add the cumin seeds and bay leaf, along with the 1 tablespoon black peppercorns and 1 tablespoon coriander seeds. Toast, shaking the pan, until fragrant, about 30 seconds. Remove from the heat and transfer to a 4-quart saucepan.

Add the cider vinegar, onion slices, garlic, sugar, and 2 tablespoons salt to the saucepan and bring to a simmer. Remove from the heat and infuse for 5 minutes. Set up a fine-mesh sieve over a bowl and pass the liquid through the strainer.

Place the mustard seeds and shredded cabbage in two separate nonreactive bowls. Pour enough pickling liquid to cover the mustard seeds, then use the remaining liquid to cover the cabbage. Place a heavy plate over the cabbage to keep it submerged. Set both aside for at least 1 hour, or until ready to use.

Remove the meat from the oven and let rest undisturbed for 1 hour at room temperature. Transfer the pastrami to a cutting board to rest. Use two forks to shred the meat and set it aside in a warm place.

Make one batch of tortillas and hold them warm.

ASSEMBLE THE TACOS: Lay out the warm tortillas on serving plates. Place some pickled cabbage on each tortilla and divide the pastrami evenly among the tacos. Top with the mustard seeds and minced onion. Squeeze a couple of the lime wedges over the tacos and serve the rest on the side.

SLAB BACON TACOS
WITH SALSA NEGRA

In this country, we have a reflexive response to anything that evokes both sweet and smoky flavors—we immediately think it tastes like barbecue. But the pleasures of pork with a sugary sauce aren't confined to the low-and-slow traditions of the United States. Salsa negra, made by soaking chipotle peppers in piloncillo syrup and frying the mixture in lard, uses Mexican techniques to rally those candied and smoldering notes so beloved to the American palate. It's thick as tar and crazy-compelling when painted on a tortilla stuffed with thick, fatty slabs of bacon.

MAKES 12 TACOS

ADVANCE PREPARATION

Salsa Negra (page 66), for serving

FOR THE FILLING

One 2-pound slab of bacon, skin removed

½ cup hulled sesame seeds

Kosher salt, as needed

TO ASSEMBLE THE TACOS

½ medium white onion, minced

2 limes, each cut into 6 wedges

1 recipe Corn or Flour Tortillas (page 35 or 41)

MAKE THE FILLING: Preheat the oven to 250°F. Set a 12-inch cast-iron skillet over medium heat for 5 minutes. Add the bacon and press to sear evenly, about 5 minutes or until well browned on the bottom. Flip the slab, then place the skillet in the oven and roast the bacon for 90 minutes. It should be deeply browned and slightly shrunken.

Remove the bacon from the oven, transfer to a plate, and let rest undisturbed for 30 minutes at room temperature. Carefully drain the accumulated fat from the skillet, reserving ¼ cup. Return the reserved fat to the skillet and heat over medium heat until it is shimmering.

Line a plate with paper towels. Add the sesame seeds to the skillet and fry until they turn a deep, golden brown, about 2 minutes. Transfer the seeds to the prepared plate and season with salt.

Make one batch of tortillas and hold them warm.

Cut the bacon slab into ¼-inch-thick slices.

ASSEMBLE THE TACOS: Lay out the warm tortillas on serving plates. Brush a thin layer of Salsa Negra on each tortilla. Evenly distribute the bacon among the tortillas and top with the sesame seeds and minced onion. Squeeze a couple of the lime wedges over the tacos and serve the rest on the side.

THE AGONY AND THE ECSTASY OF
AL PASTOR

If you've traveled through Mexico City, you've probably seen an al pastor trompo—a vertical rotisserie loaded with a hunk of pineapple and marinated pork that cooks slowly as it rotates in front of a gas flame. Shave a pile of the roasted meat into a tortilla, add a nick of the warm fruit, and you have tacos al pastor—a shawarma-like "frankenfood" that's said to have come to Mexico by way of Lebanese immigrants. Al pastor is all about that adobo-spiced meat, so rich with Maillard-reaction goodness that a single bite can short-circuit your pleasure center and leave you in a speechless, slack-jawed twilight. Not a bad way to get high.

Al pastor is my favorite taco on the planet. And also, thanks to the industrial equipment required to do it properly, it's the most difficult taco to get right. But obstacles are my Lorelei, so in 2014 I turned my obsession into an objective and decided to build an entire restaurant dedicated to al pastor tacos. To prepare for the opening of Empellón Al Pastor, I took a series of R&D trips to Mexico City, visiting taquerias. These were taco death marches that began at dawn and ended well after midnight, when we would tuck our angry, distended bellies into bed and listen to them gurgle and hiss until morning.

The tacos varied wildly. We encountered trompos dyed orange with adobo (and probably some food coloring), and trompos that seemed to have no marinade at all. Onions were diced and piled up at the foot of the spit to absorb dripping pork fat, or they were tiny cebollas charring on their own separate grid-dle. Everywhere there were salsas rojas and salsas verdes, some thickened with chunks of avocado. There were pickled onions with habanero chiles, and salt shakers, and wedges of lime—endless ways to dress and customize our tacos. At night we ate at taquerias that were auto-body shops by day, and taquerias that were staffed by teenagers chewing jícama sticks, and taquerias squeezed into market stalls next to vendors selling hula hoops and live chickens and banana leaves folded up like bed linens.

I already knew that there is no one, true way to cook or serve anything in Mexico; in D.F., I learned that's especially true of al pastor. But how to translate all of this information into a book intended for home cooks? Getting there was a long road riddled with some awesome failures. To imitate the spit-roasted texture of al pastor, my friend, the culinary technology wizard Dave Arnold, suggested that I try an archaic countertop rotisserie—a 1950s-era Roto-Broil, canonized by Jeffrey Steingarten in his book, *The Man Who Ate Everything*. I bought one on eBay, set it up, and promptly realized that the Roto-Broil is the Joe Pesci of kitchen equipment: an unpredictable and dangerous infra-red death machine, willing to impart a third-degree burn just because you looked at it funny. It was *not* the home-cook solution I'd hoped for. Next, I tried packing the marinated pork into a meatloaf pan, cooking it sous vide, searing the surface, and passing it through a meat slicer. That wasn't home-cook friendly, either. But it was fun.

Ultimately our solution was a lot simpler. It came down to distilling the hallmark pleasures of al pastor and developing a recipe—two of them, actually—that could evoke those iconic flavors and textures without exactly replicating them. The first recipe (Tacos Al Pastor, page 130) relies on a hot grill and careful knifework to achieve al pastor's gentle chew and aggressive browned-meat flavor. The second (Pineapple Lardo Tacos, page 135) contemplates the way al pastor showcases what warm, sweet fruit can do for a rich pork product. Taken on their own, each recipe is a meditation on what makes something taste distinctly like itself.

Eaten together, I think they tell the whole story.

TACOS AL PASTOR

Short of investing in a vertical broiler, this hack is the closest you'll get to al pastor tacos at home. We tend to think of pork shoulder as something that needs to be braised, but a well-butchered shoulder steak given a swift ride on a ripping hot grill can be a thing of beauty—the wide surface area means more of that good Maillard char you want from al pastor. Take your time when slicing the finished meat: thin, bias-cut slivers are the ideal texture here.

MAKES 12 TACOS

ADVANCE PREPARATION

1 cup Adobo (page 223)

Salsa Roja (page 68), for serving

Raw Salsa Verde (page 78), for serving

FOR THE FILLING

Vegetable oil, for the grill

Four ½-inch-thick boneless pork shoulder steaks (2 pounds total)

Kosher salt, as needed

TO ASSEMBLE THE TACOS

¼ ripe pineapple, peeled, cored, and cut into 24 even slices

½ medium white onion, minced

60 cilantro leaves (from about 15 sprigs), roughly chopped

2 limes, each cut into 6 wedges

1 recipe Corn or Flour Tortillas (page 35 or 41)

MAKE THE FILLING: Preheat a grill to the hottest possible setting and brush with vegetable oil. Slather about 1 cup of the Adobo all over the pork steaks and season liberally with salt.

Place the pork steaks on the hot grill and cook for 3 minutes. Rotate 45 degrees and cook for another 3 minutes. Flip and continue to cook for 3 minutes. The finished steaks should have visible charred grill marks. Remove from the grill, transfer to a plate, and set aside to rest in a warm place.

Make one batch of tortillas and hold them warm.

Cut the pork steaks against the grain and on the bias—you want the slices to be as thin as possible, almost shaved, to achieve the right tenderness and texture for al pastor.

ASSEMBLE THE TACOS: Lay out the warm tortillas on serving plates. Evenly distribute the grilled pork and the pineapple slices among the tortillas. Top with some of the Salsa Roja and Raw Salsa Verde, along with the minced onion and chopped cilantro. Squeeze a couple of the lime wedges over the tacos and serve the rest on the side.

PINEAPPLE TACOS
WITH LARDO

This variation switches up the proportions of a traditional al pastor taco. Instead of pork garnished with pineapple, this recipe calls for adobo-rubbed pineapple with wisps of lardo—a spiced and cured fatback—melting on top. You can find lardo wherever Italian salumi is sold, or at BuonItalia (see Resources). Ask your butcher to pass it through a meat slicer to get the translucent, delicate strips you'll want for this recipe.

MAKES 12 TACOS

ADVANCE PREPARATION

1 cup Adobo (page 223)

Raw Salsa Verde (page 78), for serving

Salsa Roja (page 68), for serving

FOR THE FILLING

Vegetable oil, for the grill

½ ripe pineapple, peeled, cored, and cut into 12 even slices about ½ inch thick

½ pound lardo, sliced paper-thin

TO ASSEMBLE THE TACOS

Maldon or flaky salt, as needed

½ medium white onion, minced

60 cilantro leaves (from about 15 sprigs), roughly chopped

2 limes, each cut into 6 wedges

1 recipe Corn or Flour Tortillas (page 35 or 41)

MAKE THE FILLING: Preheat a grill to the hottest possible setting and brush with vegetable oil. Slather about 1 cup of Adobo all over the pineapple pieces.

Place the pineapple pieces on the hot grill and cook for 2 minutes. Rotate 45 degrees and cook for another 2 minutes. Flip and cook for 2 minutes; rotate 45 degrees and cook for a final 2 minutes. The finished pineapple should have visible charred grill marks and the color will have deepened slightly. Remove from the grill, transfer to a plate, and set aside to rest in a warm place.

Make one batch of tortillas and hold them warm.

ASSEMBLE THE TACOS: Lay out the warm tortillas on serving plates. Place one piece of grilled pineapple on each tortilla, divide the lardo evenly among the tacos, and season with Maldon salt. Top with some Raw Salsa Verde and Salsa Roja, along with the minced onion and chopped cilantro. Squeeze a couple of the lime wedges over the tacos and serve the rest on the side.

PORK RIND TACOS
WITH MOLE VERDE

Americans tend to exalt crispy things, but rehydrating fried foods is a common technique in the Mexican kitchen—think of the softened tortillas used to make chilaquiles or the way the batter on a chile relleno is designed to soak up sauce. This taco bridges the gap between that Mexican impulse to tenderize crunch and the American instinct to preserve it. Adding chicharrones to a pot of white beans and green mole makes for a rich, bulky stew, while a garnish of the crumbled pork rinds adds just enough crackle.

MAKES 12 TACOS

ADVANCE PREPARATION

1 recipe Mole Verde (page 86)

1 recipe Cooked White Beans
   (page 227)

FOR THE FILLING

One 5-ounce bag store-bought
   pork rinds

TO ASSEMBLE THE TACOS

½ medium white onion, minced

60 cilantro leaves (from about
   15 sprigs), roughly chopped

2 limes, each cut into 6 wedges

1 recipe Corn or Flour Tortillas
   (page 35 or 41)

MAKE THE FILLING: Over a bowl, break the pork rinds into rough 1-inch pieces.

Make one batch of tortillas and hold them warm.

Set a 4-quart saucepan over a medium flame. Add the Mole Verde and beans and heat until bubbling. Add about ⅔ of the pork rinds to the saucepan, reserving the rest for garnish. Stir to combine. Remove from the heat and set aside in a warm place.

ASSEMBLE THE TACOS: Lay out the warm tortillas on serving plates. Spoon a few tablespoons of the pork rind–mole verde mixture onto each tortilla. Top with the reserved pork rinds, the minced onion, and chopped cilantro. Squeeze a couple of the lime wedges over the tacos and serve the rest on the side.

POTATO AND CHORIZO TACOS

Potato and chorizo is a staple filling at taquerias that specialize in the stewed tacos known as guisados. It makes sense; after all, crumbly sausage and diced potatoes soaked in spicy, aromatic fat is a hearty, dirt-cheap, and satisfying combination. It's also easy to make, especially if you have a batch of chorizo stowed in the freezer.

MAKES 12 TACOS

ADVANCE PREPARATION

1 recipe Red Chorizo (page 228)

Salsa de Árbol (page 65), for serving

FOR THE FILLING

1 large russet potato, peeled and diced

Kosher salt, as needed

1 tablespoon lard or vegetable oil

TO ASSEMBLE THE TACOS

1 medium white onion, minced

60 cilantro leaves (from about 15 sprigs), roughly chopped

2 limes, each cut into 6 wedges

1 recipe Corn or Flour Tortillas (page 35 or 41)

MAKE THE FILLING: Place a 2-quart saucepan over medium heat and add the diced potato and enough cold water to cover by 1 inch. Season with a small handful of salt. Bring the water to a boil, then immediately remove from the heat. Strain and transfer the potato to a plate to cool.

Set a 3½-quart Dutch oven over medium heat and add the lard. Once the fat is shimmering, add the Red Chorizo and cook until it is crumbly and has completely rendered its fat, about 15 minutes.

Add the potato to the Dutch oven and stir to combine. Continue cooking the mixture until the potato is just tender, about 10 minutes. Taste and adjust the seasoning with salt. Set aside in a warm place.

Make one batch of tortillas and hold them warm.

ASSEMBLE THE TACOS: Lay out the warm tortillas on serving plates. Evenly distribute the chorizo-potato filling among the tortillas. Top with some of the Salsa de Árbol, minced onion, and chopped cilantro. Squeeze a couple of the lime wedges over the tacos and serve the rest on the side.

SOPA SECA TACOS

In this post-Paleo dystopia, when carbs are vilified and white flour all but outlawed, stuffing a taco with pasta feels taboo. But there's something so texturally satisfying about biting through a starchy tortilla to find noodles inside, the way stuffing in a sandwich does the trick the day after Thanksgiving. The filling is actually sopa seca ("dried soup"), a Mexican dish with Spanish roots that involves simmering toasted vermicelli with broth and chorizo until all of the liquid is absorbed. For this recipe I use the smoky meat sauce Tinga Poblana (page 74) as a base, finish it with crema, and scoop it into a taco topped with crumbled queso fresco.

MAKES 12 TACOS

ADVANCE PREPARATION

1 recipe Tinga Poblana (page 74)

¾ cup Crema Mexicana (page 233)

FOR THE FILLING

½ pound dried vermicelli

1 quart lard or vegetable oil, for frying

Kosher salt, as needed

TO ASSEMBLE THE TACOS

1 cup crumbled queso fresco

½ medium white onion, minced

60 cilantro leaves (from about 15 sprigs), roughly chopped

2 limes, each cut into 6 wedges

1 recipe Corn or Flour Tortillas (page 35 or 41)

MAKE THE FILLING: Over a bowl, break the pasta into rough 2- to 3-inch pieces.

Line a plate with paper towels. Set a 5½-quart Dutch oven over medium heat and add the lard. Once the fat looks wavy, add the broken pasta pieces and fry until golden brown, about 3 minutes. Remove the pan from the heat and use a slotted spoon to transfer the fried pasta to the prepared plate.

Carefully pour the lard from the Dutch oven into a heatproof bowl. Cool and reserve for another use.

Clean the Dutch oven and set back over medium heat. Add the Tinga Poblana and bring to a simmer. Add the fried pasta, followed by ¼ cup water and return to a simmer. Cook until the pasta is just tender and most of the liquid is evaporated, about 5 minutes. Stir in the Crema Mexicana and simmer for another minute. Taste and adjust the seasoning with salt. Remove from the heat and set aside in a warm place.

Make one batch of tortillas and hold them warm.

ASSEMBLE THE TACOS: Lay out the warm tortillas on serving plates. Evenly distribute the sopa seca among the tortillas. Top with the queso fresco, minced onion, and chopped cilantro. Squeeze a couple of the lime wedges over the tacos and serve the rest on the side.

COCHINITA PIBIL TACOS

Cochinita pibil is an iconic dish of the Yucatán, as seminal to the cuisine of the peninsula as barbacoa is to Oaxaca. Just like barbacoa, cooking pork pibil involves wrapping a whole animal in banana leaves and burying it in an underground oven—a "pib"—to slow-roast for hours until the pork is fragrant and melts at the prick of a fork. The meat can then be wrapped in a tortilla, stuffed into bread for a *torta*, or served in a pool of its own broth, always with searing-hot salsa habanera and pink pickled onions on the side.

For this book, I thought it was important to show what goes into the traditional pit preparation, so turn to page 142 to see how it's done. But I stand by this home-kitchen hack as an excellent alternative if you don't want to fall down that particular rabbit hole. For this revision, I rub a pork shoulder with bright orange achiote paste, bundle it in banana leaves, and let the meat do its thing for a few hours in the oven. Other than the cooking method and some adjustments in volume to account for a whole pig rather than a shoulder, the recipes for conventional oven and earth oven pibil are identical.

MAKES 12 TACOS

ADVANCE PREPARATION

1 cup Achiote Paste (page 224)

Pickled Red Onions (page 232), for serving

Salsa Habanera (page 62), for serving

FOR THE FILLING

2 pounds boneless pork shoulder

Kosher salt, as needed

2 banana leaves

TO ASSEMBLE THE TACOS

2 limes, each cut into 6 wedges

1 recipe Corn or Flour Tortillas (page 35 or 41)

MAKE THE FILLING: Preheat the oven to 300°F. Slather 1 cup of Achiote Paste all over the pork and season liberally with salt.

Unfold the banana leaves, keeping them as intact as possible. Line the inside of a 5½-quart Dutch oven with one leaf. Lay the second leaf in the opposite direction, forming an X. The leaves should hang over the sides. Nestle the pork inside the Dutch oven. Fold the leaves over the meat and tuck in the edges. Pour in 1 cup water and cover with a lid. Cook for 3 hours or until fork-tender.

Remove the Dutch oven from the oven and let the meat rest, covered and undisturbed, for 1 hour at room temperature. Take off the lid and unfold the banana leaves. Transfer the pork to a cutting board to rest; discard the leaves.

Set up a fine-mesh sieve over a bowl and pass the cooking juices through the strainer. Clean the Dutch oven and pour the strained cooking juices back into the vessel.

Use two forks to shred the pork shoulder. Return the meat to the Dutch oven, mixing to coat it with the cooking juices. Set aside in a warm place.

Make one batch of tortillas and hold them warm.

ASSEMBLE THE TACOS: Lay out the warm tortillas on serving plates. Place a small mound of the cochinita pibil on each tortilla and top with some Pickled Red Onions. Squeeze a couple of the lime wedges over the tacos and serve the rest on the side along with the Salsa Habanera.

COCHINITA PIBIL TACOS
THE HARD WAY

They say that anything worth doing is worth doing right—or over-doing, or whatever cliché best suits your particular brand of deranged perfectionism. So, if you want to make cochinita pibil, and you have access to a backyard, a whole pig, and a moderate amount of upper-body strength, it's time to think about digging a fire pit.

In the Yucatán, they use the Mayan word *pib* to describe the earth oven used to cook cochinita pibil, turkey, and chicken. It's a simple underground hearth, lined with stones or bricks to retain the heat produced by a wood fire. The idea is to stoke the flames until the pib is uniformly hot, position whatever you're cooking on top of the embers, cover the oven, and let the residual heat work its magic. I focus on cochinita pibil here, but pit-roasting meats is pan-regional in Mexico, not limited to the Yucatán. If you go to the trouble of building a pib, you should also try firing it up for Lamb Barbacoa Tacos (page 152).

And to be clear, building a pib *is* a lot of trouble. You certainly could make this dish in an oven invented after the dawn of electricity—that's how we do it at Empellón and it isn't a bad way to go. The meat can achieve the same soft, supple texture, and the banana leaves can impart their herby aroma. But the flavor and perfume of long-smoldering wood cannot be replicated in a home kitchen, and neither can the emotional ownership that develops when you take the time to do it the ancient way. Cooking like this is an event, and not only because you'll need to invite a crowd to make a dent in the food. Unearthing a pig that's been roasting for hours underground is a little like digging up a time capsule: Every-thing is just as you left it, and yet transformed. Peeling back the banana leaves is a Thanksgiving moment. It's oohs and ahhs. It connects you and your guests to a distant time and a faraway place. It's worth doing.

I built my pib in my in-laws' backyard and cooked a 30-pound suckling pig for a crowd of about 15 (leftovers are implicit here). I walk you through it, but keep in mind that there's a certain amount of unpredictability in any cooking experience that depends so heavily on the whims of nature. Be nimble when something surprises you—weather, rooty soil, wet kindling—and have some deputies on hand to help devise a solution.

SERVES 15, WITH LEFTOVERS

ADVANCE PREPARATION

1 recipe Achiote Paste (page 224)

Pickled Red Onions (page 232), for serving

Salsa Habanera (page 62), for serving

FOR THE FILLING

1 suckling pig, 30–45 pounds*

Kosher salt, as needed

5 banana leaves, plus more as needed

TO ASSEMBLE THE TACOS

10 limes, each cut into 6 wedges

5 recipes Corn or Flour Tortillas (page 35 or 41)

EQUIPMENT: One 18 by 24 by 6-inch roasting pan; butcher's twine; 4 stakes; 2 or more shovels; 70 red clay bricks; 5 bundles of firewood; kindling; heat-safe gloves or oven mitts; two 36-inch pieces of aluminum sheeting; broom

*You'll need to place a special order with your butcher to reserve a whole pig. Ask him or her to break down the animal into 2 hams, 2 shoulders, 1 head, and 1 saddle. Your butcher can either separate the feet from the hind- and forequarters or leave them attached. Either way these pieces should fit nicely in an even layer in your roasting pan. If you are in the mood to butcher the pig yourself, have fun and don't worry too much about perfection here. It's all going to get picked from the bone and shredded anyway.

PREPARE THE PIB: The first thing you'll need to do is choose a place to dig your pib. The fire will give off smoke, and the ground will heat up significantly, so you want the pit to be a safe distance from your home, in an area that doesn't get a lot of foot traffic.

The size of your pit should be based on the size of your roasting pan. You want at least 6 inches of ventilation clearance around and on top of the pan, taking into account about 4 extra inches on each side for the bricks and the bed of embers. Our pan was 18 inches wide, 24 inches long, and 6 inches deep, so we planned for a 38 by 44 by 16-inch pit.

Use twine and stakes to mark off the dimensions; I used my mother-in-law's "I ♥ Jesus" pencils but you don't have to—and be careful to map out a tidy rectangle. The bricks are geometrically perfect, so if the hole is uneven, they won't align. (You'll quickly realize, as I did, that it's nigh impossible to dig a perfect rectangle unless you're Rain Man. You may then throw a brief but potent tantrum as your pregnant wife and co-author look on from the patio, smirking into their donuts. This is fine. It will all work out.)

Line the bottom of the pit with bricks first and then build up the sides, taking care to make the walls of your inevitably lopsided rectangle as seamless

recipe continues

as possible—the bricks act as insulation, and gaps allow the heat to escape. Now sound the trumpets: You've got a pib.

PREPARE THE FIRE: I was a total pyro when I was a kid, so this is the fun part. First, take a second to get super-excited about the fact that you're about to light a big, freaking fire and it's going to crackle and burn and be awesome. Fire, fire, fire!

Criss-cross about six fat logs in the pib with some kindling underneath and light it up. The blaze should get pretty big, and you want to keep it roaring for a good 4 hours before it burns down to all coals. Here, you're creating your own pint-size Hades, ensuring that the heat retained by the bricks and surrounding earth will be enough to cook an entire beast. If you're as lucky as I am, your in-laws' neighbor will see this moment as a perfect opportunity to show off his new sound system, and begin blasting the smooth, sweet sounds of Kenny G. Appoint someone to keep the fire burning; this is your cue to head inside.

PREP THE PIG: Follow the instructions on page 141 to season the pig parts with achiote paste and salt, and assemble the banana leaf casserole. Since you're preparing a whole pig rather than just a shoulder, you'll need more kosher salt than the conventional recipe requires, so have about 1 cup on hand—and more of the achiote paste (the full recipe on page 224 will suffice for a suckling pig).

Depending on the size of your pan, you'll also need more banana leaves; for my pan, I used 5: 2 leaves to lay lengthwise and 3 to cover the width.

Once you've assembled the roasting pan, leave it out to come to room temperature so that it doesn't rob the fire's heat once you place it in the pib. Now, you just need to wait on that fire. This would be a good time to prep the Pickled Red Onions (page 232) and Salsa Habanera (page 62). Or you could just drink some mezcal and glower at the neighbor who has still not quit it with the fucking Kenny G.

COOK THE PIG: The oven is ready when an even bed of embers has developed—about 6 inches deep and covered with a layer of gray ash. For us, this took about 4 hours. Now, it's time to bury the pig.

Wear a pair of heat-safe gloves or oven mitts as you lower the roasting pan into the center of the pib. Once it is in position, lay a brick on each corner of the pan to keep it anchored in place. Then pour in some water to create steam and ensure that the meat doesn't scorch. The waterline should come up at least 3 inches from the bottom of the pan—for us that was about a gallon of water.

NOW IT'S GO-TIME: You need to work quickly to snuff out the flames while trapping their heat. Position the pieces of sheet metal over the oven, covering

recipe continues

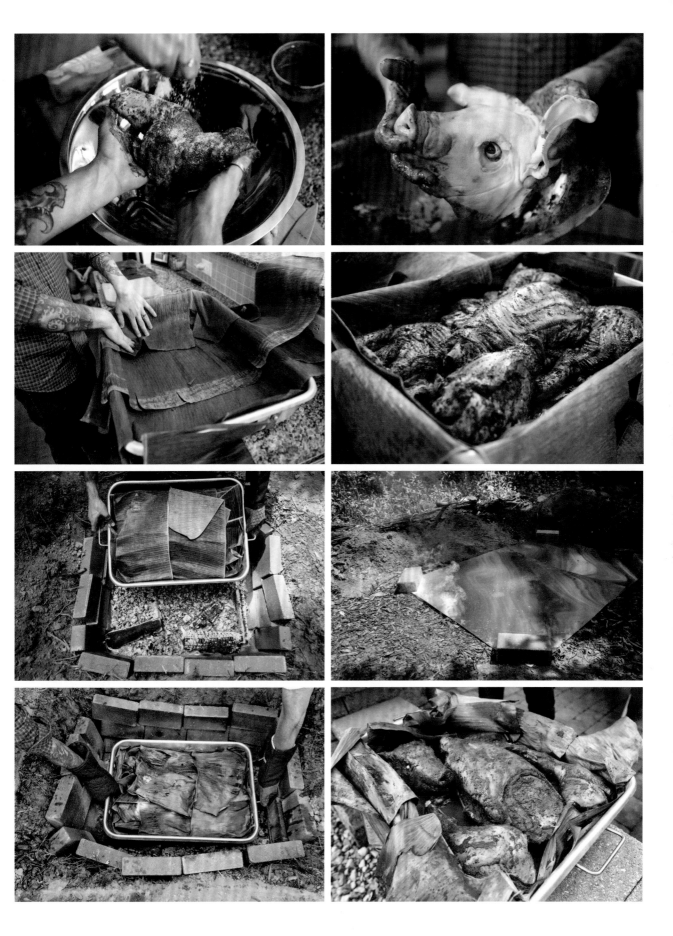

it completely, and immediately begin shoveling soil on top. Bury the perimeter first to prevent the lid from buckling, and then work toward the center. Keep your eyes peeled for plumes of escaping smoke; these indicate that the fire inside is still getting enough oxygen to burn. Cover those spots with more soil.

Once the oven is fully buried and there is no visible smoke, you can walk away. You must leave the pib undisturbed for at least 4 hours, but you could safely let it go for as long as 12 hours. With the water regulating the heat and all that bone, skin, and cartilage protecting the pork, it's not that easy to overcook the meat.

You've got some downtime. Drink some, sleep some. Watch *Boogie Nights* a few times. Memorize Dirk Diggler's rendition of *The Touch*. Make some side dishes. Slow-simmered Black Ayocote Beans (page 226) would be delicious finished with a few ladles of the pibil pan drippings.

About an hour before you plan to dig up the pig, start making the tortillas. You'll need a lot of them to feed a crowd—about 60, or five batches of the Corn Tortilla recipe (page 35) should do it. Keep them wrapped in a slightly moist towel inside a casserole dish in a 200°F oven until showtime.

UNEARTH THE PIG: The quiet horror of this moment cannot be overstated. You're going to

dig this thing up, and all of your friends and family are going to watch it happen. Maybe it's going to be perfect, or maybe the heat dissipated too early and you've basically just disinterred a raw pig corpse, and you've ruined Christmas or whatever. The point is, there's a lot on the line.

Begin by gently shoveling aside the dirt pile on top of the oven. When you've cleared most of it away, switch to a broom and sweep the lid—you don't want any of the soil falling into the roasting pan when you lift the metal sheeting. Brace yourself. Remove the lid.

It should smell good. Like really good. First, you'll get all those herbal tea notes from the steamed banana leaves, and then the warm wood perfume of the embers. Hoist the roasting pan from the pib and set it on a side table. Peel

back the banana leaves and you'll see that the pork skin has stiffened and browned, and the achiote paste has deepened in color, from rust to mahogany, and there's murky *jus* swirled with pork fat pooling in the bottom of the pan. It's a good scene.

Carve the pork away from the bone and shred it into a clay cazuela or other serving dish. Add some of the broth to the cazuela to keep the meat moist, save a few ladles of it to add porky richness to the simmering ayocote beans, if you've made them. Set up the cochinita pibil and the stack of warm tortillas next to bowls of Pickled Red Onions, Salsa Habanera, the lime wedges, and the side of beans.

Then, let people assemble their own goddamned tacos because that's fun and because—come on, buddy—you've done enough.

CARNITAS TACOS

Carnitas, like Louisiana gumbo or Northeastern lobster rolls, is a highly personal and regionalized dish with infinite variations. I've seen carnitas started in milk, like blanquette de veau, or finished in the deep fryer with all the pomp of a mozzarella stick. I've seen carnitas prepared using a tidy, trimmed pork shoulder, or an organs-and-all whole pig to impart that deep, mineral flavor only offal can provide. For my purposes, I define carnitas simply as meat that's been slow-cooked and then crisped in its own fat. I serve these with a sweet salsa verde marmalade— just a raw verde thickened with pectin and sugar—that offers both the bright flavor of fresh herbs and the jammy intensity of cooked-down fruit.

MAKES 12 TACOS

ADVANCE PREPARATION

1 recipe Raw Salsa Verde (page 78)

FOR THE SALSA VERDE MARMALADE

2 cups sugar

4 teaspoons apple pectin powder

2 tablespoons fresh lime juice

FOR THE FILLING

1 tablespoon dried Mexican oregano

One 4-inch stick of canela (Mexican cinnamon)

40 garlic cloves, skins on

1 cup kosher salt

6 tablespoons fresh lime juice

One 2-pound piece boneless pork shoulder

6 cups lard, melted

TO ASSEMBLE THE TACOS

½ medium white onion, minced

60 cilantro leaves (from about 15 sprigs), roughly chopped

2 limes, each cut into 6 wedges

1 recipe Corn or Flour Tortillas (page 35 or 41)

MAKE THE SALSA VERDE MARMALADE: Place the Raw Salsa Verde in a medium saucepan. Mix the sugar and pectin in a small bowl, then stir into the saucepan. Fit the saucepan with a candy thermometer and set over medium heat. Bring the mixture to a boil, then turn the heat down and simmer gently until the thermometer registers 222°F, about 20 minutes. Remove the marmalade from the heat and transfer to a bowl. Add the 2 tablespoons lime juice and stir to combine. Let cool to room temperature; the mixture will begin to thicken as it cools. Transfer to a container and refrigerate until ready to use. (The marma-

lade will keep for up to 3 months in the refrigerator; use any excess as a glaze for roasted meats or spread it on toast and eat it with avocado.)

MAKE THE FILLING: Set a 12-inch cast-iron skillet over medium heat for 5 minutes. Add the oregano and canela and toast, shaking the pan, until fragrant, about 15 seconds. Remove from the heat, transfer to a spice grinder, and grind to a fine powder.

Reheat the skillet over medium heat. Add the garlic cloves and roast, turning them from time to time, until softened slightly and blackened in spots, about 6 minutes. Turn off the heat, remove the garlic from the skillet, and set it aside to cool at room temperature. Once they are cool enough to handle, peel the garlic cloves and discard the skins.

In a food processor, combine the ground spices and the roasted garlic, along with the salt and the 6 tablespoons lime juice. Process

the mixture to a paste, transfer to a bowl, and set aside until ready to use.

Preheat the oven to 250°F. Place the pork shoulder on a large rimmed tray and slather the spice rub all over it. Let sit for 30 minutes. (Alternatively, you can season the pork 1 day ahead and refrigerate overnight.)

Drain off any liquid that has accumulated in the tray. Rinse the shoulder under cold running water and pat dry with paper towels. Nestle the pork shoulder in a 5½-quart Dutch oven. Pour the melted lard over the shoulder and cover with a lid. Place in the oven and cook for 4 hours or until fork-tender.

Remove the Dutch oven from the oven and let rest undisturbed for 1 hour at room temperature. Transfer the pork shoulder to a plate and carefully drain the lard from the Dutch oven, reserving ½ cup. Pour the reserved lard back into the Dutch oven and set over high heat until the fat is shimmering.

Return the pork shoulder to the Dutch oven and sear for about 3 minutes on all sides, or until well browned. Remove from the heat and use two forks to shred the carnitas, mixing to coat with the hot lard. Cover the pot, and set aside in a warm place.

Make one batch of tortillas and hold them warm.

ASSEMBLE THE TACOS: Lay out the warm tortillas on serving plates. Place a tablespoon of the marmalade on each tortilla, followed by some of the carnitas. Top with minced onion and chopped cilantro. Squeeze a couple of the lime wedges over the tacos and serve the rest on the side.

DUCK CARNITAS TACOS

The preparation of the French bistro classic duck confit is nearly identical to that of Mexican carnitas. This taco puts a fine point on that cross-cultural rapport, swapping pork for poultry that's rubbed in Mexican aromatics and slow-simmered in lard. The skin browns up so beautifully in the final step that the finished meat eats almost like duck chicharrones.

MAKES 12 TACOS

ADVANCE PREPARATION

Roasted Salsa Verde (page 80), for serving

FOR THE SPICE RUB

1 tablespoon dried Mexican oregano

One 4-inch stick of canela (Mexican cinnamon)

40 garlic cloves, skins on

1 cup kosher salt

6 tablespoons fresh lime juice

FOR THE FILLING

6 duck legs (about 3 pounds)

6 cups lard, melted

TO ASSEMBLE THE TACOS

½ medium white onion, minced

60 cilantro leaves (from about 15 sprigs), roughly chopped

2 limes, each cut into 6 wedges

1 recipe Corn or Flour Tortillas (page 35 or 41)

MAKE THE SPICE RUB AND FILLING: Set a 12-inch cast-iron skillet over medium heat for 5 minutes. Add the oregano and canela and toast, shaking the pan, about 15 seconds. Transfer to a spice grinder and grind to a fine powder.

Reheat the skillet. Add the garlic cloves and roast, turning them from time to time, until softened slightly and blackened in spots, about 6 minutes. Turn off the heat, remove the garlic from the skillet, and set aside to cool at room temperature. Once cool enough to handle, peel the garlic and discard the skins.

In a food processor, combine the ground spices, roasted garlic, the salt and lime juice. Process the mixture to a paste, transfer to a bowl, and set aside.

Preheat the oven to 250°F. Place the duck legs on a tray and slather the spice rub all over them. Let sit for 30 minutes. (Alternatively, you can season the duck a day ahead and refrigerate overnight.)

Drain off any liquid that has accumulated in the tray. Rinse the legs under cold running water and pat dry. Nestle the duck into a 5½-quart Dutch oven. Pour the melted lard over the legs and cover. Place in the oven and cook for 4 hours, or until fork-tender.

Remove the Dutch oven from the oven and let rest undisturbed for 1 hour at room temperature. Transfer the duck legs to a plate and carefully drain the lard from the Dutch oven, reserving ½ cup.

Pick the meat from the bones, chopping the skin and folding it into the meat. Pour reserved lard into the Dutch oven and set over high heat until shimmering.

Return the meat to the Dutch oven and sear untouched until browned. Stir the duck and continue to cook, stirring, until uniformly crispy. Remove the Dutch oven from the heat and use two forks to shred the duck, mixing to coat it with the hot lard. Cover the pot, and set aside in a warm place.

Make one batch of tortillas and hold them warm.

ASSEMBLE THE TACOS: Lay out the warm tortillas on serving plates. Divide the carnitas evenly among the tortillas and top with some of the Roasted Salsa Verde, minced onion, and chopped cilantro. Squeeze a couple of the lime wedges over the tacos and serve the rest on the side.

BEER-BRAISED TONGUE TACOS
WITH SALSA DE ÁRBOL

This is one of my favorite tacos, and it has been a fixture at Empellón Taqueria since we opened our doors. It falls into the category of a taco de guisado—typically a stewed meat or vegetable filling that can be easily rewarmed and scooped into a tortilla. The filling is sturdy by design, so this taco would hold up well for a dinner party. Serve it in cold weather: the filling has all the comforting qualities of a stew, with a lively edge derived from the spiced red chorizo.

Note that I call for *pork* tongue here, rather than the more common beef tongue. I find it easier to work with because it requires very little peeling—most of the thin skin dissolves as it braises and you just pick away whatever bits remain after it cooks. You could use beef tongue, but you'll need to take that extra step of peeling it carefully after it braises.

MAKES 12 TACOS

ADVANCE PREPARATION

1 cup Red Chorizo (page 228)

Salsa de Árbol (page 65), for serving

FOR THE FILLING

2 cups diced slab bacon (about ¾ pound)

2 medium white onions, thinly sliced

6 garlic cloves, minced

Three 12-ounce bottles lager-style beer

1½ pounds pork tongues (about 3 whole tongues)

2 medium Idaho potatoes

1 tablespoon kosher salt

TO ASSEMBLE THE TACOS

6 ounces queso fresco, crumbled

2 limes, each cut into 6 wedges

1 recipe Corn or Flour Tortillas (page 35 or 41)

MAKE THE FILLING: Set a 6-quart stockpot over medium heat and add the bacon. Cook until the fat has rendered and the bacon is browned, about 5 minutes. Add the onions and garlic and cook, stirring, until the onions begin to brown on the edges. Add the Red Chorizo and cook until crumbly, about 5 minutes. Pour the beer into the pot and nestle the pork tongues in the mixture—they should be submerged in the beer. Bring to a simmer and reduce the heat to maintain a gentle simmer. Cover the pot and cook for 4 hours.

Remove the stockpot from the heat and transfer the pork tongues to a plate. Cool the tongues in the refrigerator for 30 minutes.

Meanwhile, peel and dice the potatoes. Set the stockpot with the chorizo mixture back over medium heat and add the potatoes.

Bring to a simmer and cook until the potatoes are tender, about 20 minutes.

Remove the tongues from the refrigerator. Peel away any remaining skin and discard. Medium-dice the tongues and add them to the stockpot to warm. Season the stew with salt and set it aside in a warm place.

Make one batch of tortillas and hold them warm.

ASSEMBLE THE TACOS: Lay out the warm tortillas on serving plates. Evenly distribute the tongue stew among the tortillas and top with crumbled queso fresco and some Salsa de Árbol. Squeeze a couple of the lime wedges over the tacos and serve the rest on the side.

LAMB BARBACOA TACOS
WITH SALSA BORRACHA

I read a story once about a Mexican immigrant cook who would drive the thousands of miles between New York City and Puebla just to keep her Bronx restaurant stocked with the right chiles, spices, and herbs. That's an insane thing to contemplate in a convenience culture such as ours: Why not work with what you have—make a substitution or cut a corner? Then you taste something like an avocado leaf and it starts to make sense.

Avocado trees are in the laurel family, and their aromatic leaves are used like bay leaves—to season stews and braises—but in greater quantities. Their anise-like flavor is one of those faint but cardinal distinctions that make some Mexican dishes hard to replicate in the United States. Before I opened Empellón Taqueria, I was hoarding 15 kilos of the stuff in my Brooklyn apartment. The point is that avocado leaves aren't the easiest ingredient to track down, but going the extra mile pays dividends when you're making Oaxacan lamb barbacoa. I've had luck finding the dried leaves at Mexican and Asian markets (pick up frozen banana leaves for this recipe while you're there) and through various online vendors.

The good news is that once you've tracked down the ingredients and prepped the adobo, this barbacoa is pretty simple to cook. You could go the traditional route and dig a pit to cook it underground over white-hot embers, just like the cochinita pibil described on page 142. But a long, slow ride in a low-temperature oven does the trick to impart the leaves' heady aroma. I like to serve this barbacoa with olives and Salsa Borracha (page 81), a tomatillo sauce punched up with a shot of mezcal.

MAKES 12 TACOS

ADVANCE PREPARATION

1 cup Adobo (page 223)

Salsa Borracha (page 81), for serving

FOR THE FILLING

2 pounds boneless lamb shoulder

Kosher salt, as needed

2 banana leaves

2 cups loosely packed dried avocado leaves

TO ASSEMBLE THE TACOS

1 small cucumber, thinly sliced

24 green olives, such as picholine or manzanilla, pitted and finely chopped

½ medium white onion, minced

60 cilantro leaves (from about 15 sprigs), roughly chopped

2 limes, each cut into 6 wedges

1 recipe Corn or Flour Tortillas (page 35 or 41)

MAKE THE FILLING: Preheat the oven to 300°F. Slather the Adobo all over the lamb shoulder and season liberally with salt.

Gently unfold the banana leaves, keeping them as intact as possible. Line the inside of a 5½-quart Dutch oven with one banana leaf. Lay the second leaf across it in the opposite direction, forming an X. The leaves should hang over the sides.

Arrange 1 cup of the avocado leaves in a single layer on the bottom of the pot. Nestle the lamb shoulder in the casserole, and top with the remaining avocado leaves. Fold the banana leaves over the meat and tuck in the edges. Pour in 1 cup water and cover with a lid. Place in the oven and cook for 3 hours, or until fork-tender.

Remove the Dutch oven from the oven and let rest, covered and undisturbed for 1 hour at room temperature. Take off the lid and unfold the banana leaves. Transfer the lamb to a cutting board to rest. Pick off any avocado leaves clinging to the meat and discard along with the banana leaves.

Set up a fine-mesh sieve over a bowl and pass the cooking juices through the strainer. Clean the Dutch oven and pour the strained cooking juices into the vessel.

Use two forks to shred the lamb shoulder. Return the meat to the Dutch oven, mixing to coat it with the cooking juices. Set aside in a warm place.

Make one batch of tortillas and hold them warm.

ASSEMBLE THE TACOS: Lay out the warm tortillas on serving plates. Divide the barbacoa evenly among the tortillas and drizzle with some Salsa Borracha. Top with the sliced cucumber, chopped green olives, minced onion, and chopped cilantro. Squeeze a couple lime wedges over the tacos and serve the rest on the side.

LAMB TARTARE TACOS

This barbacoa riff is an exercise in reversal. The tartare simulates the flavors and preserves the soul of the slow-cooked Oaxacan staple, but what was once cooked is now raw and what was once hot is now cold. Into a mince of lamb loin goes avocado-leaf–infused oil and some guajillo-based salsa roja. A garnish of guaje seeds—umami-rich kernels from pods of the Leucaena tree—intensifies the gamey flavor.

MAKES 12 TACOS

ADVANCE PREPARATION

2 tablespoons Salsa Roja
    (page 68)

Salsa Borracha (page 81), for
    serving

FOR THE AVOCADO LEAF OIL

1 pasilla Oaxaqueño chile, stemmed

2 cups loosely packed dried
    avocado leaves

½ cup vegetable oil

FOR THE FILLING

1½ pounds boneless lamb loin,
    trimmed of all fat and sinew

1 teaspoon kosher salt

TO ASSEMBLE THE TACOS

12 raw guaje pods, seeds removed,
    husks discarded

½ medium white onion, minced

60 cilantro leaves (from about
    15 sprigs), roughly chopped

2 limes, each cut into 6 wedges

1 recipe Corn or Flour Tortillas
    (page 35 or 41)

MAKE THE AVOCADO LEAF OIL: Set a 12-inch cast-iron skillet over medium heat for 5 minutes. Add the pasilla Oaxaqueño chile and toast, turning from time to time until you see the first wisp of smoke, about 30 seconds. Transfer the chile to a bowl.

Working in batches, add the avocado leaves to the skillet and toast briefly until fragrant, about 15 seconds. Turn off the heat and transfer the leaves to the bowl with the chile.

Place the chile and avocado leaves in a blender along with the vegetable oil and puree on high speed until the leaves are pulverized. Set up a fine-mesh sieve over a bowl and pass the oil through the strainer. Set aside.

MAKE THE FILLING: With a very sharp chef's knife, cut the meat across the grain into very thin slices and then cut the slices into thin strips. Mince the meat into a fine tartare and transfer to a bowl.

Add the 2 tablespoons Salsa Roja and ¼ cup of the avocado leaf oil to the tartare and mix thoroughly. Season with salt. Refrigerate until ready to use.

Make one batch of tortillas and hold them warm.

ASSEMBLE THE TACOS: Lay out the warm tortillas on serving plates. Divide the lamb tartare evenly among the tortillas and spread using the back of a spoon. Top with some of the Salsa Borracha, and the guaje seeds, minced onion, and chopped cilantro. Squeeze a couple of the lime wedges over the tacos and serve the rest on the side.

GOAT TACOS
WITH SAVORY CAJETA

Cajeta is a ubiquitous sweet treat in Mexico—a fudgy reduction of goat's milk and sugar that's often drizzled on pastries or sandwiched between Mexican wafer cookies. Intrigued by the idea of cooking goat meat in its own milk, I created a savory version of cajeta, steeped in onions and meat *jus*. Although it was a Mexican food that inspired this, the end result doesn't offer a particularly Mexican flavor profile. Fight that instinct to throw cilantro on it and call it a fiesta. This taco eats like a classic European braise, so it gets a classical garnish of thyme.

Note that I use goat shoulder and leg for variety here, but you could use two shoulders or two legs, depending on what is available.

MAKES 12 TACOS

FOR THE FILLING

1 small bone-in goat shoulder
(about 2½ pounds)

1 small bone-in goat leg (about
2½ pounds)

Kosher salt and freshly ground
black pepper, as needed

¼ cup lard or vegetable oil

1 medium white onion, thinly sliced

2 quarts goat's milk

TO ASSEMBLE THE TACOS

Maldon or flaky salt and freshly
ground black pepper, as needed

½ medium white onion, minced

2 tablespoons fresh thyme leaves

2 limes, each cut into 6 wedges

1 recipe Corn or Flour Tortillas
(page 35 or 41)

MAKE THE FILLING: Preheat the oven to 250°F. Season the goat shoulder and leg liberally with salt and pepper.

Set a 5½-quart Dutch oven over high heat and add the lard. When the fat begins to smoke, add the goat meat, working in two batches if necessary. Sear the pieces until golden brown all over, about 10 minutes total. Transfer the goat to a plate and set aside.

Add the onion slices to the Dutch oven and cook, stirring, until translucent. Pour in the goat's milk and bring to a simmer. Nestle the goat meat in the Dutch oven and cover with a lid. Place in the oven and cook for 2½ hours, or until fork-tender. Remove the Dutch oven from the oven and transfer the goat to a cutting board to rest.

Set a fine-mesh sieve over a bowl and pass the braising liquid through the strainer.

Set a 4-quart saucepan over low heat and add the strained cooking liquid. Simmer until reduced to 1 cup, stirring occasionally, about 90 minutes. The liquid will turn a light caramel color and be slightly thickened. Taste and season with salt, if necessary.

Use two forks to shred the goat meat off the bone. Add the meat to the saucepan, mixing to coat it with the savory cajeta. Set aside in a warm place.

Make one batch of tortillas and hold them warm.

ASSEMBLE THE TACOS: Lay out the warm tortillas on serving plates. Place a small mound of the shredded goat in savory cajeta on each tortilla. Season with salt and pepper, and top with minced onion and thyme leaves. Squeeze a couple of the lime wedges over the tacos and serve the rest on the side.

A NOTE ON
TRIPE

Maybe you're squeamish about cooking with tripe—a cow's honeycomb-like stomach lining—so let me make my case up front. It's easy enough to throw a tenderloin in a pan with some butter and declare it delicious, but refining and transforming an off-cut into something that anyone would want to eat is a measure of skill and a matter of pride. When it is prepared properly, tripe can provide one of the most haunting tastes and textures in all of gastronomy; it is soft, lush, and a little grassy, saturated with the flavors of whatever it's been simmered in.

But like anything else, preparing tripe correctly takes time and effort. Unprocessed tripe is naturally brown, with bits of hay and other digestive detritus stuck to it. Much of the tripe you get in the United States is already bleached, so you aren't likely to encounter that, but you'll still want to take the time to clean and deodorize it so it gives up some of its funk. The salt and lime juice in this recipe serve that purpose, and the blanching step scours it further. Once the tripe is clean, getting it tender is just about patience. Let it simmer in the menudo until softened, with just enough chew to remind you of what you're eating.

TRIPE TACOS
WITH MENUDO REDUCTION

The mystical hangover cure known as *menudo* performs its necromancy on the recently drunk all over Mexico, especially in Guadalajara. But the traditional tripe soup is magnificent whether or not you're treating a day-after delirium. To turn menudo into a taco, we simmer tripe with a pig's foot to give the broth an extra boost of meaty, gelatinous intensity, then let the liquid reduce to concentrate its flavors. We finish the chewy ragout with menudo's traditional garnishes: a flurry of radish, cabbage, and minced onion.

MAKES 12 TACOS

ADVANCE PREPARATION

Salsa de Árbol (page 65), for serving

FOR THE FILLING

1½ pounds honeycomb tripe (see page 158)

½ cup kosher salt

Juice from 2 limes

10 guajillo chiles

1 teaspoon dried Mexican oregano

1 teaspoon cumin seeds

10 garlic cloves, skins on

1 pig's foot

TO ASSEMBLE THE TACOS

¼ large head of green cabbage, shredded

1 radish, sliced into thin rounds

½ medium white onion, minced

2 limes, each cut into 6 wedges

1 recipe Corn or Flour Tortillas (page 35 or 41)

PREPARE THE TRIPE: Place the tripe in a large bowl; cover with the salt and the lime juice. Place in the refrigerator and allow to marinate for 30 minutes.

Remove the tripe from the refrigerator, drain, and rinse under cold running water. Set a 6-quart stockpot over medium heat and add the tripe and enough cold water to cover by a few inches. Bring to a boil, then immediately remove from the heat and transfer the tripe to a large bowl. Rinse the tripe once again under cold running water and transfer to a cutting board.

Slice the tripe so that it lays flat against the cutting board. Medium-dice the tripe and refrigerate until ready to use.

MAKE THE FILLING: Remove the stems from the guajillo chiles and tear the chiles open. Shake out and discard the seeds. Remove and discard the veins. Tear the chiles into small pieces.

Set a 12-inch cast-iron skillet over medium heat for 5 minutes. Add the oregano and toast briefly until fragrant, about 15 seconds. Set aside. Add the cumin seeds to the skillet and toast, shaking the pan, until fragrant. Remove from the heat, transfer to a spice grinder, and grind to a fine powder. Transfer to a bowl.

Reheat the skillet over medium heat. Add the guajillo chile pieces and toast, turning from time to time, until you see the first wisp of smoke, about 30 seconds. Transfer to the spice grinder and grind to a fine powder.

Add the garlic cloves to the skillet and roast, turning them from time to time, until softened slightly and blackened in spots, about 6 minutes. Turn off the heat, remove the garlic from the skillet, and set aside to cool at room temperature. Once they are cool enough to handle, peel the garlic cloves and discard the skins.

Clean the stockpot and set over medium heat. Add the tripe and pig's foot along with enough water to cover by a few inches and bring to a simmer.

Meanwhile, place the roasted garlic, ground cumin, and chiles in a blender along with 2 cups of the simmering liquid from the stockpot. Puree on high speed until completely smooth. Set a fine-mesh sieve over a bowl and pass the puree through the strainer. Pour the mixture into the stockpot with the tripe and pig's foot and simmer for 3 hours.

Remove the pot from the heat. Transfer the tripe to a bowl and let cool in the refrigerator. Discard the pig's foot.

Set the stockpot back over medium heat and bring the broth to a simmer. Cook until reduced by half, skimming the froth from the surface with a ladle, about 45 minutes. Taste and adjust the seasoning with salt.

Remove the tripe from the refrigerator and place it back in the stockpot to warm.

Make one batch of tortillas and hold them warm.

ASSEMBLE THE TACOS: Lay out the warm tortillas on serving plates. Distribute the menudo evenly among the tortillas and top with the shredded cabbage, radish slices, toasted oregano, and a drizzle of Salsa de Árbol. Squeeze a couple of the lime wedges over the tacos and serve the rest on the side.

FAVA AND BLOOD SAUSAGE TACOS
WITH MINT SALSA VERDE

Unlike Spanish morcilla (often spiked with paprika and oregano) or the fennel pollen and winter spice flavors of Italian biroldo, Oaxacan blood sausage—sangrita—is prominently seasoned with mint. The herb provides a freshness that's surprising in the context of intense, mineral-rich blood sausage, and it's a pretty delicious detour. Sangrita and potato is a common taco filling, but I like the idea of using fava beans when they are in season. The beans mimic the potato's starchiness, while their nutty green flavor is a perfect layup for a salsa verde that swaps the usual cilantro for more bracing mint. The finished taco is a high-wire act: Deep flavors balance bright ones, and fresh, snappy vegetables enliven the sangrita's sticky texture, all in the same satisfying bite.

MAKES 12 TACOS

ADVANCE PREPARATION

1 recipe Blood Sausage (page 229)

Raw Salsa Verde (page 78), substituting cilantro with mint, for serving

FOR THE FILLING

¼ cup extra-virgin olive oil

2½ pounds fresh fava beans, shucked, blanched, and peeled (1½ cups)

1 teaspoon kosher salt

TO ASSEMBLE THE TACOS

36 mint leaves (from about 6 sprigs), cut into chiffonade

2 limes, each cut into 6 edges

1 recipe Corn or Flour Tortillas (page 35 or 41)

MAKE THE FILLING: Set a 12-inch sauté pan over medium heat and add the olive oil. Once the oil is shimmering, add the Blood Sausage and break apart using a wooden spoon. Cook until the sausage is dark and rendered, about 5 minutes. Add the fava beans and cook until warm. Season with salt. Remove from the heat and set aside in a warm place.

Make one batch of tortillas and hold them warm.

ASSEMBLE THE TACOS: Lay out the warm tortillas on serving plates. Evenly distribute the sausage-bean mixture among the tortillas and top with some of the Mint Salsa Verde and the mint chiffonade. Squeeze a couple of the lime wedges over the tacos and serve the rest on the side.

FISH TEMPURA TACOS

I've heard legends about how crispy fish tacos became a religion in Baja: that Japanese fishermen docked in the region and married their tempura traditions to the available Mexican ingredients. But however it came to be that fried fish met crunchy cabbage and cool mayo on a tortilla doesn't matter all that much to me—it's just an awesome taco.

At the restaurants, we use dogfish, a small school shark known as cazón in Mexico. But the beauty of this taco is in its flexibility; just about any light-flavored, white-fleshed fish will perform well. It's the batter that makes or breaks a good fried-fish taco, and this one is dialed in. The key is not to overwork it: mix the batter too much, and you'll start developing the flour's gluten, which will make for a chewy crust. And keep the batter cold, as you would a pie dough; store it in the refrigerator until the last possible moment, for the best results.

MAKES 12 TACOS

ADVANCED PREPARATION

Roasted Salsa Verde (page 80), for serving

FOR THE FILLING

1½ pounds boneless, skinless white fish fillet, such as bass, snapper, or cod

3⅓ cups rice flour

1¼ cups all-purpose flour

1 teaspoon baking powder

One 12-ounce bottle lager-style beer, cold

2½ quarts (10 cups) vegetable oil, for frying

Kosher salt, as needed

TO ASSEMBLE THE TACOS

¾ cup mayonnaise

¼ head of green cabbage, shredded

4 radishes, sliced into thin rounds

½ medium white onion, minced

60 cilantro leaves (from about 15 sprigs), roughly chopped

2 limes, each cut into 6 wedges

1 recipe Corn or Flour Tortillas (page 35 or 41)

PREPARE THE FISH AND BATTER:
Portion the fish into 12 even pieces, each about 3 inches long. Store in the refrigerator until ready to use.

In a large bowl, mix 1⅓ cups of the rice flour with the all-purpose flour and baking powder. Pour the beer into the bowl and whisk gently. Don't overwork the batter; a few lumps are okay. Place the batter in the refrigerator until ready to use.

Place a 5½-quart Dutch oven fitted with a candy thermometer over medium heat and add the vegetable oil, leaving at least 3 inches of space between the surface of the oil and the lip of the pot. Heat until the thermometer registers 350°F.

Make one batch of tortillas and hold them warm.

FRY THE FISH: Line a plate with paper towels and sprinkle the remaining 2 cups rice flour on a separate plate. Remove the fish pieces from the refrigerator and season all over with salt.

Remove the tempura batter from the refrigerator. Dredge the fish in the rice flour and then dip the pieces into the batter, one by one. Carefully add each piece of fish to the hot oil. Work in small batches so as to not crowd the Dutch oven. Fry the fish until golden brown, about 3 minutes. Transfer to the prepared plate and season immediately with more salt.

ASSEMBLE THE TACOS: Lay out the warm tortillas on serving plates. Place 1 tablespoon of mayonnaise on each tortilla and spread using the back of a spoon. Add a small mound of the cabbage, along with some radish slices, minced onion, chopped cilantro, and a spoonful of Roasted Salsa Verde. Place one piece of fried fish on each tortilla. Squeeze a couple of the lime wedges over the tacos and serve the rest on the side.

GRILLED ARCTIC CHAR TACOS
WITH CAPE GOOSEBERRY SALSA

Come summer, you need a light grilled fish taco in your recipe arsenal as sure as you need SPF. This one does nicely, with meaty, crisp-skinned arctic char and tart cape gooseberries that pop in your mouth like beads of roe. Try the same recipe with swordfish, tuna, trout, or bass.

MAKES 12 TACOS

ADVANCE PREPARATION

Cape Gooseberry Salsa (page 83), for serving

Crema Mexicana (page 233), for serving

FOR THE FILLING

Vegetable oil, for the grill

Two 18-ounce arctic char fillets, skin on

¼ cup extra-virgin olive oil

Kosher salt, as needed

TO ASSEMBLE THE TACOS

24 cape gooseberries, each sliced in half

½ medium white onion, minced

60 cilantro leaves (from about 15 sprigs), roughly chopped

2 limes, each cut into 6 wedges

1 recipe Corn or Flour Tortillas (page 35 or 41)

MAKE THE FILLING: Preheat a grill to a medium-hot setting and brush with vegetable oil. Check the fillet for any remaining bones and discard. Portion the fish into 12 even pieces. Coat the fish with the olive oil and season with salt.

Place the fish on the grill skin side down and cook for 2 minutes. Rotate 45° and cook for 1 minute. Flip and continue to cook for 2 minutes. The finished fish should be just beginning to flake, with visibly charred grill marks. Carefully remove the fish from the grill, transfer to a plate, and set aside to rest in a warm place.

Make one batch of tortillas and hold them warm.

ASSEMBLE THE TACOS: Lay out the warm tortillas on serving plates. Place one piece of grilled fish, skin side up, on each tortilla and drizzle with Cape Gooseberry Salsa and Crema Mexicana. Top with the halved gooseberries, minced onion, and chopped cilantro. Squeeze a couple of the lime wedges over the tacos and serve the rest on the side.

THE TYRANNY OF
CHEAP EATS

In the corporate world, there's a term for the intangible impasse that keeps minorities and women out of upper management positions. They call it a "glass ceiling." In the food world, we have similar issues: racial and gender disparity in professional kitchens and, relevant to this book, a real problem with the way we think about and value "ethnic" cooking. We don't have a term for this yet—for this habit of paying handsomely for certain cuisines while exiling others to a cheap eats ghetto. I can think of one, though. I'm gonna call it bullshit.

When we opened Empellón Taqueria, we were selling trios of tacos for $16 and taking a beating for that. Tacos, we were told, should cost two bucks and anything else is "inauthentic." That rankled. At Empellón, we pay the same rates for the same ingredients as any fine-dining temple. You can buy a scallop in its shell, shuck it, sear it, baste it in butter, and sell it in midtown for $24. But put the same product on a tortilla and suddenly the cost does not compute. Charging prices that reflected our sourcing made us a target. No matter what they're stuffed with, our critics seemed to suggest, tacos just aren't worth as much as other foods.

This isn't unique to Mexican food. We think of French cuisine as luxurious, worthy of a high price tag. The cuisines of most other Western European countries and that of Japan enjoy the same esteem. But then there's the Middle East, India, many Asian countries, and most of Latin America. There are a handful of restaurants in the United States that fight the current, but I don't think

I'm overstating it when I say that we tend to think of the food of these regions as "divey." Sure, there are plenty of pavement-pounding Andrew Zimmern and Anthony Bourdain acolytes who exalt *pani puri* and *xiao long bao*. But for most of us, it's street food, drunk food, college food. We've vulgarized it to such an extent that we're actually offended when a restaurant comes along that tries to shift the paradigm.

I can't tell you how many times I've been accused of posturing as the white knight of Mexico. That I'm trying to save a coarse cuisine from itself with my magic Anglo fairy dust. Or that the food I cook is a rip-off because someone's roommate knows of a place in East Harlem that serves the same stuff for a song. There's nothing wrong with cheap tacos, mind you, but it's not what I'm doing. I don't believe in putting a cap on what Mexican food is worth. And frankly, who are we to decide which cuisines are worthy of opulence and which are not?

The thing is, good ingredients matter in

any cuisine. Good ingredients cost money, good talent costs money, building a beautiful restaurant that sends a message about the food you're about to eat—that costs money. All of this has an impact on your tab, and if you're of the opinion that Mexican food must always be cheap, you're not going to support a place that doesn't fall in line. Thus begins a nasty game of dominoes. We can make Mexican food cheaper, but the pork won't come from those small Pennsylvania farms you like and the tortillas won't be handmade anymore because we can't afford to pay someone to prep them throughout service. The menu won't be as intriguing because we won't be able to attract the same caliber of chef without enough buying power for a fair salary, great equipment and the best raw materials. Melted cheese, ground beef, and tortilla chips are pretty cheap though, so at least now the price is right. Bleak.

So here's what I'm going to ask of you. If you'd happily shell out for slow-cooked lamb at some farm-to-table American restaurant, then give a barbacoa taco the same opportunity to impress. If you'd order duck confit at a brasserie without fretting when the bill comes, then try approaching pork carnitas—cooked just like confit in its own luscious fat—with the same open mind. If you'd throw a foodie conniption over seared scallops at Jean Georges, try eating the same preparation on a tortilla and see what you think (that recipe follows). But mostly I'm asking you to ditch the idea that Mexican cuisine, that any cuisine actually, has to abide by some blue book valuation that cuts it off at the knees. I've discovered as much rigor and range cooking Mexican food as I ever found thumbing through *Le Guide Culinaire*. I've tasted sauces that number their ingredients in double digits, count their cook time in days, and possess a flavor so vast and mystifying it borders on psychotropic. I've eaten tortillas that are as careful and calibrated as any crusty *ficelle*. To brand a cuisine with such bottomless complexity "cheap" is to support an ethnocentric appraisal system that entirely misses the point. It's wrong. It's ugly. It's a missed opportunity.

I guess it's true that you get what you pay for.

SCALLOP TACOS JGV

The idea that a taco can be as serious and sublime as any composed, haute-cuisine dish informs the work I do at all of my restaurants, and certainly in this book. To make that point, I decided to prepare an iconic Jean-Georges Vongerichten dish and serve it on a tortilla at Empellón Cocina. This scallop preparation helped make JGV's flagship restaurant a sensation when it opened in 1997, and it's just as brilliant in a taco. The buttery puree of capers, golden raisins, and sherry vinegar is an excellent salsa for the golden florets of sautéed cauliflower and seared sweet scallops.

MAKES 12 TACOS

FOR THE CAPER-RAISIN EMULSION

½ cup brined capers, drained and rinsed

¼ cup golden raisins

6 tablespoons (¾ stick) unsalted butter

1 teaspoon sherry vinegar

1 teaspoon kosher salt

Freshly ground black pepper

FOR THE FILLING

4 tablespoons vegetable oil

4 tablespoons (½ stick) unsalted butter

Eight 1½-inch cauliflower florets, quartered lengthwise into ¼-inch slices (24 pieces)

12 jumbo sea scallops (about 1½ pounds)

Kosher salt and freshly ground black pepper, as needed

TO ASSEMBLE THE TACOS

¼ teaspoon freshly grated nutmeg

12 parsley leaves (from about 2 sprigs), cut into chiffonade

1 recipe Corn or Flour Tortillas (page 35 or 41)

MAKE THE EMULSION: Set a 1-quart saucepan over low heat and add the capers, raisins, and ¾ cup water. Bring to a simmer and cook until the raisins plump, about 10 minutes. Transfer to a blender and puree on high speed. With the blender running, add the 6 tablespoons butter 1 tablespoon at a time, making sure each is incorporated before the next is added. Add the sherry vinegar and season with salt and black pepper. Continue to blend until completely smooth. Set aside.

Make one batch of tortillas and hold them warm.

MAKE THE FILLING: Set a 12-inch sauté pan over medium-high heat and add 1 tablespoon vegetable oil and 1 tablespoon butter. Once the butter is melted, add half the cauliflower slices and cook for 2½ minutes. Flip and cook for another 2½ minutes, until the cauliflower is just tender and lightly browned. Transfer to a plate and season with salt. Repeat the cooking process with 1 tablespoon each vegetable oil and butter and the remaining cauliflower slices.

Season the sea scallops with salt and black pepper. Clean the sauté pan and set it back over medium-high heat with 1 tablespoon vegetable oil and 1 tablespoon butter. Once the butter is melted, add 6 of the scallops and cook until golden brown on the bottom, about 3 minutes. Do not flip. Transfer the scallops to a plate, reserving the pan juices. Repeat the process with the remaining 1 tablespoon each vegetable oil and butter and the remaining 6 scallops. Slice the scallops in half horizontally.

ASSEMBLE THE TACOS: Lay out the warm tortillas on serving plates. Drizzle a tablespoon of the caper-raisin emulsion over each tortilla. Shingle 2 slices of cauliflower between 2 slices of scallop on each tortilla and finish with some of the pan sauce. Top with a sprinkling of nutmeg and the parsley leaves.

BAY SCALLOP CEVICHE TACOS
WITH COCOA VINAIGRETTE

Chocolate plays an important role in Mexican cuisine, but it's typically used to add depth and richness to heavier recipes, as in a Mole Poblano. When I first prepared this dish during an *Iron Chef* battle against Cat Cora in 2008, I liked how I was able to make dark, bitter cocoa nibs and powder work in a lighter context. Tempered with lime juice, this chocolate vinaigrette is an intriguing dressing for gumdrop-sweet bay scallops and serrano chiles. The avocado also takes on a new role here; seasoning it with sugar brings out the fruit's natural banana-like sweetness. Sugar, fruit, and chocolate—after all, I was a pastry chef once.

MAKES 12 TACOS

FOR THE AVOCADO PUREE

2 Haas avocados

1 tablespoon fresh lime juice

1 tablespoon sugar

1½ teaspoons kosher salt

FOR THE FILLING

1 tablespoon cocoa nibs

2 teaspoons Dutch-process cocoa powder

3 tablespoons fresh lime juice

2 teaspoons sugar

3 tablespoons extra-virgin olive oil

1½ pounds bay scallops

½ medium white onion, minced

1 serrano chile, thinly sliced

½ teaspoon kosher salt

TO ASSEMBLE THE TACOS

Maldon or flaky salt, as needed

60 cilantro leaves (from about 15 sprigs), roughly chopped

2 limes, each cut into 6 wedges

1 recipe Corn or Flour Tortillas (page 35 or 41)

MAKE THE AVOCADO PUREE: Cut open the avocados, remove their pits, and scoop the flesh into a blender. Add the 1 tablespoon lime juice, 1 tablespoon sugar, and 1½ teaspoons salt, and puree on high speed until completely smooth. Set aside.

MAKE THE FILLING: Set a 12-inch cast-iron skillet over medium heat for 5 minutes. Toast the cocoa nibs briefly, shaking the pan, until fragrant, about 15 seconds. Remove from the heat and set aside.

In a small bowl, mix the cocoa powder with the 3 tablespoons lime juice and 2 teaspoons sugar, and whisk. Pour the olive oil into the mixture and stir gently, making sure not to emulsify it.

In a separate bowl, mix the bay scallops with the minced onion and serrano chile. Season with the ½ teaspoon salt and refrigerate until ready to use.

Make one batch of tortillas and hold them warm.

ASSEMBLE THE TACOS: Lay out the warm tortillas on serving plates. Place a tablespoon of avocado puree on each tortilla and spread using the back of a spoon. Evenly distribute the bay scallop ceviche among the tortillas and drizzle with the cocoa vinaigrette. Season with Maldon salt and top with the toasted cocoa nibs and chopped cilantro. Squeeze a couple of the lime wedges over the tacos and serve the rest on the side.

FRIED OYSTER TACOS
WITH SALSA RAVIGOTE

I grew up in a part of Massachusetts where drive-up seafood shacks outnumber Walmarts, and there's only one sensible way to eat anything plucked from the ocean: deep fried and dunked in tartar sauce. When I worked at Clío in Boston, I discovered that the French have a fancier name for that combination of mayo, relish, and spices: *sauce ravigote*. Come on; it's tartar sauce.

But whatever, okay, we'll do it your way, France. Rather than a scoop of Heinz sweet relish, this ravigote is seasoned with cornichons, tarragon, shallots, and Dijon mustard. There's absolutely nothing Mexican about this "salsa"—or the crunchy fried oysters it's paired with. But the flavor takes me right back to the hood of my Chevy Beretta parked in the dusty lot outside Jackie's Dairy Bar, with a paper basket of crunchy, warm bivalves in my hands. Nothing wrong with that.

MAKES 12 TACOS

FOR THE SALSA RAVIGOTE

3 tablespoons sherry vinegar

1 tablespoon Dijon mustard

½ cup vegetable oil

½ cup fresh tarragon, chopped

¼ cup fresh parsley, chopped

¼ cup brined capers, drained and chopped

¼ cup cornichons, chopped

¼ cup shallots, minced

3 hard-boiled eggs, chopped

FOR THE FILLING

2 cups all-purpose flour

3 cups panko bread crumbs, plus more as needed

6 large eggs, beaten

Kosher salt, as needed

24 oysters, shucked and drained

2½ quarts (10 cups) vegetable oil, for frying

TO ASSEMBLE THE TACOS

¾ cup mayonnaise

1 head of frisée lettuce, cored and leaves separated

2 radishes, sliced into thin rounds

1 bunch of chives, finely chopped

1 recipe Corn or Flour Tortillas (page 35 or 41)

MAKE THE SALSA RAVIGOTE: In a small bowl, mix the sherry vinegar, mustard, ½ cup vegetable oil, tarragon, parsley, capers, cornichons, shallots, and hard-boiled eggs. Set aside.

PREPARE THE OYSTERS: To create a breading station, line up three wide, shallow bowls or pie plates. Fill the first bowl with the all-purpose flour; the second with 3 cups bread crumbs, and the third with the beaten eggs. Season the flour and eggs with salt.

Working 3 at a time, dredge the oysters in the flour and gently shake off any excess. Next, dip in the egg wash. Finally, transfer the oysters to the bowl with the bread crumbs and lightly press to coat evenly; you may need to replenish the bread crumbs as you work. Transfer to a clean plate and place in the refrigerator until ready to cook.

Make one batch of tortillas and hold them warm.

FRY THE OYSTERS: Place a 5½-quart Dutch oven fitted with a candy thermometer over medium heat and add the 2½ quarts vegetable oil, leaving at least 3 inches of space between the surface of the oil and the lip of the pot. Heat until the thermometer registers 350°F. Line a plate with paper towels.

Remove the breaded oysters from the refrigerator. Carefully add them to the hot oil, working in small batches so as to not crowd the Dutch oven. Fry the oysters until golden brown, about 1 minute. Transfer to the prepared plate and season with salt.

ASSEMBLE THE TACOS: Lay out the warm tortillas on serving plates. Place a tablespoon of mayonnaise on each tortilla, followed by a tablespoon of the salsa ravigote, taking care to use the solid herbs. Spread using the back of a spoon. Place 2 fried oysters on each taco, and top with some of the frisée leaves, radish slices, and chopped chives. Squeeze a couple of the lime wedges over the tacos and serve the rest on the side.

GRILLED SHRIMP TACOS
WITH PIPIÁN

Dieselboy, né Damian Higgins, is a world-famous drum and bass DJ who crash-landed on my radar when I was seventeen and heard him spin at a Boston rave. Years later, I discovered that he's also an opinionated food fanatic and an obsessive home cook with a taste for complicated, rococo recipes. Our mutual fanboy bonhomie eventually turned into a close friendship. These tacos grew out of an idea Damian pitched: pairing light, sweet shrimp with the hearty complexity of pipián. The sauce is a kind of gateway mole, made with pumpkin and sesame seeds, seasoned with achiote, árbol chiles, and tons of toasted spices, and cooked down in a few inches of ripping-hot lard. Pipián is labor-intensive, but the work is easy to defend when you taste what the stuff can do for a simple pile of grilled shrimp. This one's for you, Dieselboy.

MAKES 12 TACOS

ADVANCE PREPARATION

Pipián (page 93), for serving

FOR THE FILLING

½ cup raw, hulled, unsalted pepitas (pumpkin seeds)

Vegetable oil, for the grill

36 jumbo shrimp (about 1½ pounds), peeled and deveined

¼ cup extra-virgin olive oil

Kosher salt, as needed

TO ASSEMBLE THE TACOS

1 Haas avocado, cut into 12 slices lengthwise

½ medium white onion, minced

60 cilantro leaves (from about 15 sprigs), roughly chopped

2 limes, each cut into 6 wedges

1 recipe Corn or Flour Tortillas (page 35 or 41)

MAKE THE FILLING: Set a 12-inch cast-iron skillet over medium heat for 5 minutes. Toast the pepitas until golden brown, shaking the pan frequently to prevent them from burning, about 30 seconds. Remove from the heat and transfer to a bowl.

Preheat a grill to the hottest possible setting and brush with vegetable oil. In a large bowl, combine the shrimp with the olive oil and season with salt.

Place the shrimp on the hot grill and cook for 1 minute. Flip and cook for another minute, or until just cooked through. Remove the shrimp from the grill, transfer to a plate, and set aside to rest in a warm place.

Make one batch of tortillas and hold them warm.

ASSEMBLE THE TACOS: Lay out the warm tortillas on serving plates. Evenly distribute the avocado and shrimp among the tortillas. Top with a generous drizzle of the Pipián, pepitas, the minced onion, and chopped cilantro. Squeeze a couple of the lime wedges over the tacos and serve the rest on the side.

LOBSTER TACOS
WITH SWEET CORN ESQUITES

Stationed along promenades, plazas, and busy byways all over Mexico are street vendors stirring pots of esquites—kernels of field corn warmed in an epazote-scented broth, then scooped into plastic cups and dressed with lime, mayo, and Cotija cheese. This taco captures those flavors using seasonal sweet corn and an epazote-infused mayo. And because corn and shellfish is a no-brainer combination for a son of New England, I've added lobster to the mix here, too.

The recipe calls for chile piquín powder, a common finishing touch for esquites. If you can't find it in the ethnic aisle at your grocery store, substitute another variety of chile powder, like ancho or guajillo.

MAKES 12 TACOS

FOR THE EPAZOTE MAYONNAISE

¾ cup mayonnaise

20 epazote leaves (from about 3 branches)

FOR THE FILLING

1 tablespoon lard or vegetable oil

6 árbol chiles

6 garlic cloves, peeled

3 ears of sweet corn, shucked, kernels cut off the cobs

Kosher salt, as needed

Two 1½-pound lobsters, boiled, shucked, meat cut into chunks

TO ASSEMBLE THE TACOS

1 cup crumbled Cotija cheese

1 teaspoon chile piquín powder

2 limes, each cut into 6 wedges

1 recipe Corn or Flour Tortillas (page 35 or 41)

MAKE THE EPAZOTE MAYONNAISE: In a blender, combine the mayonnaise and epazote leaves and puree on high speed until completely smooth. Set aside.

MAKE THE FILLING: Set a 12-inch sauté pan over high heat and add the lard. Once the fat is smoking, add the árbol chiles and garlic cloves and cook until browned, about 1 minute.

Lower the heat to medium, add the corn kernels, and cook undisturbed until the kernels begin to brown, about 3 minutes. Shake the pan and continue cooking the corn undisturbed for another 3 minutes. It should be seared and evenly coated with fat.

Add 1 cup water to the sauté pan and season with salt. Cook until the corn is tender and most of the liquid has evaporated, about 5 minutes.

Pick out the árbol chiles and garlic cloves, and discard. Add the lobster meat to the sauté pan and heat until warm.

Make one batch of tortillas and hold them warm.

ASSEMBLE THE TACOS: Lay out the warm tortillas on serving plates. Place a tablespoon of epazote mayonnaise on each tortilla and spread using the back of a spoon. Evenly distribute the lobster-corn esquites among the tortillas and top with the Cotija cheese and chile piquín powder. Squeeze a couple of the lime wedges over the tacos and serve the rest on the side.

CRAB CAKE TACOS
WITH CHILPACHOLE

The bubbly chilpachole foam that finishes this taco is a tip of the hat to the halcyon days of modernist cooking. That was a simpler time—a time before we all knew about the stabilizing wonders of lecithin, Versawhip, and methylcellulose. When all you needed to make a foam was stock, butter, an immersion blender, and zero ethical hang-ups about ripping off Charlie Trotter. Those were the days, am I right?

Of course, it hardly needs saying that in Mexico chilpachole isn't a foam. It's a crab soup that originated in Veracruz, where blue crabs—jaiba—are everywhere, skittering along the shoreline or trussed up in knotted palm fronds at the fish markets. This crab cake taco reimagines that soup in the context of my modernist pastry background and my New England appetite for picked shellfish.

MAKES 12 TACOS

ADVANCE PREPARATION

1 recipe Crab Broth (page 231)

FOR THE CHILPACHOLE

3 plum tomatoes

12 garlic cloves, skins on

6 chipotle morita chiles

1 tablespoon lard or vegetable oil

1 epazote branch

1 tablespoon unsalted butter

FOR THE FILLING

1 pound lump crab meat

¾ cup mayonnaise

3 tablespoons fresh lime juice

1 teaspoon freshly ground black pepper

1 canned chipotle chile, minced

12 epazote leaves (from about 2 branches), finely chopped

4½ cups panko bread crumbs

2 teaspoons kosher salt, plus more as needed

2 cups all-purpose flour

6 large eggs, beaten

2 cups vegetable oil

1 recipe Corn or Flour Tortillas (page 35 or 41)

BEGIN THE CHILPACHOLE: Preheat the broiler. Roast the tomatoes on a baking sheet until blackened in spots, 5 to 6 minutes. Turn them over and continue to blacken, another 5 to 6 minutes. Remove from the broiler and set aside to cool at room temperature. Once they are cool enough to handle, peel the tomatoes and discard the skins.

Set a 12-inch cast-iron skillet over medium heat for 5 minutes. Add the garlic cloves and roast, turning them from time to time, until softened slightly and blackened in spots, about 6 minutes. Remove the garlic from the skillet and set aside to cool at room temperature. Once they are cool enough to handle, peel the garlic cloves and discard the skins. Set aside with the tomatoes.

Reheat the skillet over medium heat. Toast the chipotle morita

recipe continues

chiles, turning from time to time, until you see the first wisp of smoke, about 30 seconds. Transfer the chiles to a bowl, cover with hot tap water, and place a heavy plate over the chiles to keep them submerged. Set aside to soak for 30 minutes.

Drain the soaked chiles and discard the liquid. Remove and discard the stems and seeds.

Place the roasted tomatoes, garlic, and chipotle morita chiles in a blender and puree on high speed until completely smooth. Set aside.

Set a 4-quart saucepan over medium heat. Add the lard and heat until smoking. Pour in the puree all at once; it will sputter. Lower the heat to a simmer and stir the puree with a wooden spoon as you cook it down to a thick, dark paste, about 5 minutes.

Add the Crab Broth and epazote branch to the saucepan and bring to a simmer. Cook until reduced by half, about 45 minutes.

MEANWHILE, MAKE THE CRAB CAKES: In a bowl, combine the crab meat, mayonnaise, lime juice, black pepper, canned chipotle, epazote leaves, 1½ cups of the bread crumbs, and 2 teaspoons salt; mix gently so as to not break up the crab meat. Divide the mixture into 12 equal patties and set on a plate.

Line up three wide, shallow bowls or pie plates. Fill the first bowl with the flour, the second with the remaining 3 cups bread crumbs, and the third with the beaten eggs. Season the flour and eggs with salt.

Working one at a time, dredge each crab cake in the flour and gently shake off any excess. Next, dip in the egg wash. Finally, transfer the crab cake to the bowl with the bread crumbs and lightly press to coat evenly. Transfer to a clean plate and place in the refrigerator until ready to cook.

Make one batch of tortillas and hold them warm.

COOK THE CRAB CAKES: Line a plate with paper towels. Set the cast-iron skillet over medium heat. Add the 2 cups vegetable oil and heat until shimmering. Working in batches of 4, cook the crab cakes until golden brown on the bottom, about 2 minutes. Flip and cook for another 1½ minutes. Transfer to the prepared plate and season with salt.

FINISH THE CHILPACHOLE: Transfer the chilpachole to a 1-quart saucepan. Add the butter and tilt the saucepan toward you. Using a hand blender, pulse until frothy and foamy.

ASSEMBLE THE TACOS: Lay out the warm tortillas on serving plates. Place a crab cake on each tortilla and top with skimmed-off spoonfuls of the chilpachole foam.

BAKED SKATE TACOS
WITH SALSA VERACRUZ

I wage a quiet war with myself when a recipe seems too easy. The hours and effort that go into barbacoa, the elaborate architecture of a Mole Poblano—these are occasions to evangelize about the virtues of Mexican cuisine and how gravely abridged our knowledge of it really is. But then a taco like this baked skate number comes along, and it doesn't want anything to do with that rhapsodic crap. In fact, it doesn't really want to make much of a point at all; it's just a delicious, simple way to deliver mellow fish and the Spanish-tinged flavors of Salsa Veracruz from hand to mouth. The skate becomes ropy as it cooks, absorbing the salsa so that each bite tastes of capers and olives, toasted spices, and fresh parsley.

MAKES 12 TACOS

ADVANCE PREPARATION

1 recipe Salsa Veracruz (page 73)

FOR THE FILLING

4 skate wings (about 2 pounds)

¼ cup extra-virgin olive oil

Kosher salt and freshly ground
   black pepper, as needed

TO ASSEMBLE THE TACOS

2 limes, each cut into 6 wedges

1 recipe Corn or Flour Tortillas
   (page 35 or 41)

MAKE THE FILLING: Preheat the oven to 300°F. Portion the skate wings into 12 even pieces. Rub the fish with olive oil and season liberally with salt and pepper.

Carefully roll the skate pieces into cylinders and place them on a baking sheet, cut side down. Spoon about 3 cups of the Salsa Veracruz over the skate, reserving the remaining salsa. Place in the oven and cook for about 30 minutes, or until fork-tender.

Remove from the oven and let rest undisturbed for 10 minutes at room temperature.

Make one batch of tortillas and hold them warm.

ASSEMBLE THE TACOS: Lay out the warm tortillas on serving plates. Place a baked skate wing on each tortilla and top with some of the reserved Salsa Veracruz.

SMOKED SALMON TACOS
WITH SALMON ROE SALSA

When I venture into nontraditional tacos at Empellón, it's hard to know exactly where to draw the line. I'm constantly asking myself if some outré creation I've dreamed up feels natural or is rooted in a Mexican idea, or if it teeters on appropriation. When I do cross cultural borders at the restaurant I tend to take cues from what's around me or what I grew up with—the foods of New England, where I'm from; the flavors of my Italian-American childhood home; and the culinary touchstones of New York City, where I live and cook now. The last is the idea behind this taco, a nod to the Jewish delicatessens and appetizing shops of lower Manhattan, with cream cheese, lox, and beads of salty salmon roe.

MAKES 12 TACOS

FOR THE SALMON ROE SALSA

1 plum tomato, diced small

1 serrano chile, thinly sliced

½ medium white onion, minced

1 tablespoon fresh lime juice

8 ounces salmon roe

FOR THE FILLING

One 8-ounce package cream
  cheese, room temperature

2 tablespoons fresh lime juice

12 ounces thinly sliced smoked
  salmon

TO ASSEMBLE THE TACOS

1 small cucumber, thinly sliced

60 cilantro leaves (from about
  15 sprigs), roughly chopped

2 limes, each cut into 6 wedges

1 recipe Corn or Flour Tortillas
  (page 35 or 41)

MAKE THE SALMON ROE SALSA: In a bowl, combine the plum tomato, serrano chile, onion, 1 tablespoon of lime juice, and salmon roe; stir gently. Transfer to a container and refrigerate until ready to use.

MAKE THE FILLING: In a stand mixer fitted with the paddle attachment, combine the cream cheese and 2 tablespoons of lime juice. Mix until the cream cheese is completely smooth and spreadable. Transfer to a container and set aside until ready to use.

Make one batch of tortillas and hold them warm.

ASSEMBLE THE TACOS: Lay out the warm tortillas on serving plates. Place a tablespoon of lime cream cheese on each tortilla and spread using the back of a spoon. Evenly distribute the smoked salmon among the tortillas and top with the cucumber slices, a spoonful of salmon roe salsa, and the chopped cilantro. Squeeze a couple of the lime wedges over the tacos and serve the rest on the side.

SEA URCHIN GUACAMOLE TACOS
WITH SEA URCHIN SALSA

This taco was born out of a shared opinion among my cooks and friends that a tortilla is as worthy of precious ingredients as any piece of Raynaud china. When I thought about making a sea urchin taco, I knew that working it into guacamole would magnify the briny sweetness the spiky creature is known for—the fat in an avocado can help stretch and carry flavors just like a knob of butter. Its lobes (sometimes called "tongues") show up three times in this taco: mashed with avocado, piled on top of the guacamole in a bright orange heap, and combined with chipotle and lime juice in a simple salsa.

The sea urchin and avocado have a similar luscious texture, and biting into this taco is a bit like face-planting into a just-fluffed pillow or planting a raspberry on a fat baby's belly. It's over the top opulent, the kind of celebratory dish that everyone deserves an occasion to eat. When the time comes, you'll need a ton of urchin—156 tongues. Many fishmongers and Japanese grocers (who call them uni) sell them pre-shucked by the tray, so you won't have to mess with those spiky shells.

MAKES 12 TACOS

FOR THE SEA URCHIN SALSA

36 sea urchin tongues

3 canned chipotle chiles, minced

1½ teaspoons sugar

1 tablespoon fresh lime juice

Maldon or flaky salt, as needed

FOR THE FILLING

2 Haas avocados

½ medium white onion, minced

1 serrano chile, minced

3 tablespoons fresh lime juice

60 cilantro leaves (from about 15 sprigs), roughly chopped

Maldon or flaky salt, as needed

72 sea urchin tongues

TO ASSEMBLE THE TACOS

48 sea urchin tongues

Maldon or flaky salt, as needed

½ medium white onion, minced

60 cilantro leaves (from about 15 sprigs), roughly chopped

2 limes, each cut into 6 wedges

1 recipe Corn or Flour Tortillas (page 35 or 41)

MAKE THE SEA URCHIN SALSA: In a small bowl, combine the 36 sea urchin tongues with the chipotles, sugar, 1 tablespoon lime juice, and Maldon salt. Use a fork to gently crush the ingredients together. Transfer to a container and refrigerate until ready to use.

MAKE THE FILLING: Cut open the avocados, remove their pits, and scoop the flesh into a bowl. Add the ½ minced white onion, serrano chile, 3 tablespoons lime juice, chopped cilantro, Maldon salt, and 72 sea urchin tongues. Use a fork or an avocado masher to gently mash the guacamole and set aside.

Make one batch of tortillas and hold them warm.

ASSEMBLE THE TACOS: Lay out the warm tortillas on serving plates. Place a few tablespoons of the sea urchin guacamole on each tortilla and evenly distribute the 48 urchin tongues among the tacos. Season with salt and top with the sea urchin salsa, minced onion, and chopped cilantro. Squeeze a couple of the lime wedges over the tacos and serve the rest on the side.

SHISHITO PEPPER TACOS

This simple taco is an adaptation of rajas con crema—typically, strips of poblano peppers simmered in cream. Rajas is one of those Mexican dishes that seems uncanny in the way it extracts so much flavor from so few ingredients; roasting, steaming, and peeling the poblanos gives the stew a charred, earthy quality. Subbing in shishitos is a small tweak that saves time and subtly alters the flavor. The Japanese peppers are grassier than poblanos, with a variable heat level. And because they don't need to be roasted and peeled (their skin is too thin for that), the finished taco has more of that raw pepper bite. Keep an eye on the shishitos while they're cooking, and pull them from the heat while they still have some of their bright green color.

MAKES 12 TACOS

FOR THE FILLING

2 tablespoons dried Mexican oregano

1 tablespoon lard or vegetable oil

4 garlic cloves, minced

1 medium white onion, thinly sliced

1 tablespoon kosher salt

3 cups heavy cream

¾ pound shishito peppers, stemmed and cut into quarters lengthwise

TO ASSEMBLE THE TACOS

2 limes, each cut into 6 wedges

1 recipe Corn or Flour Tortillas (page 35 or 41)

MAKE THE FILLING: Set a 12-inch cast-iron skillet over medium heat for 5 minutes. Add the oregano and toast briefly, shaking the pan until fragrant, about 15 seconds. Set aside.

Set a 12-inch sauté pan over medium heat and add the lard. Once the fat is shimmering, add the garlic and cook until golden brown. Add the onion, season with salt, and cook until translucent. Pour in the cream, reduce the heat to a low simmer, and cook until the cream has thickened enough to coat the back of a spoon, about 30 minutes.

Add the shishito peppers and oregano to the pan and cook until they are slightly wilted but have not yet turned army green, about 10 minutes. Remove from the heat and set aside in a warm place.

Make one batch of tortillas and hold them warm.

ASSEMBLE THE TACOS: Lay out the warm tortillas on serving plates. Evenly distribute the shishito pepper mixture among the tortillas. Squeeze a couple of the lime wedges over the tacos and serve the rest on the side.

PICO DE GALLO TACOS

This summery taco is inspired by what we call Salsa Mexicana (page 70) in this book, but you might know it better as pico de gallo—a raw salsa made with tomato, serrano chiles, cilantro, and onion. There's not much to it, and that's kind of the point: A taco can be an event, an all-day cooking project, or just be a simple way to showcase and enjoy seasonal produce when it is at its peak. Tomatoes are their juiciest in the Northeast around August, and I can't imagine a better way to eat them than wrapped in a tortilla with a little salt, some chile pepper heat, and bright herbs. I find that beefsteaks have exactly the right texture and water content to hold up on a tortilla without getting soggy, but a beautiful heirloom tomato would be great, too.

MAKES 12 TACOS

FOR THE FILLING

6 ripe beefsteak or heirloom
   tomatoes (about 1½-2 pounds)

Maldon or flaky salt, as needed

1 medium white onion, minced

60 cilantro leaves (from about
   15 sprigs), roughly chopped

2 serrano chiles, thinly sliced

TO ASSEMBLE THE TACOS

2 limes, each cut into 6 wedges

1 recipe Corn or Flour Tortillas
   (page 35 or 41)

MAKE THE FILLING: Slice the top and bottom off each tomato and discard. Halve the tomatoes vertically and then cut across into ½-inch-thick slices.

Make one batch of tortillas and hold them warm.

ASSEMBLE THE TACOS: Lay out the warm tortillas on serving plates. Evenly distribute the tomato slices among the tortillas and season with salt. Top with minced onion, chopped cilantro, and the serrano chile slices. Squeeze a couple of the lime wedges over the tacos and serve the rest on the side.

CHILE RELLENO TACOS
WITH SALSA RANCHERA

Whenever I read a menu at a Mexican restaurant in America, I'm struck by how thoroughly our appetite for all things golden, brown, and delicious has imposed itself. If all you knew of Mexican cooking was what you learned at a Señor Frog's, no one could blame you for thinking that the country's cuisine hinges on having a Fryolator. But generally speaking, Mexicans don't share that loyalty to crunchy stuff. Their fried foods are often submerged in sauce, then served and eaten quickly while the dish hovers in that textural purgatory between crispy and soggy. It might seem like the only appropriate thing to do with a gorgeously fried poblano pepper that's stuffed with molten Chihuahua cheese is to shove it promptly into your mouth. But take a beat; try giving that chile relleno a warm bath in salsa ranchera, until the batter is just soaked through. Fold it into a tortilla, and eat the oozing thing in a few ravenous bites.

MAKES 12 TACOS

ADVANCE PREPARATION

1 recipe Salsa Ranchera (page 72)

FOR THE FILLING

6 poblano chiles

2 cups grated Chihuahua cheese

6 large eggs, separated

1 tablespoon kosher salt, plus more as needed

2¼ cups all-purpose flour

2½ quarts (10 cups) vegetable oil, for frying

TO ASSEMBLE THE TACOS

½ medium white onion, minced

2 limes, each cut into 6 wedges

1 recipe Corn or Flour Tortillas (page 35 or 41)

START THE FILLING: Preheat the broiler. Roast the poblano chiles on a baking sheet until blackened in spots, about 3 minutes. Turn them over and continue to blacken for another 3 minutes. Remove from the broiler and transfer to a bowl. Cover tightly with plastic wrap and let the chiles steam for 10 minutes.

Cut off the tops of the chiles 1 inch from the stems and carefully peel off and discard the skins. Line a plate with paper towels. Cut the chiles in half lengthwise and rinse under cold running water to remove any seeds or remaining skin. Transfer to the prepared plate and pat dry.

Lay the chiles flat on a cutting board, skin side down. Divide the Chihuahua cheese evenly among the chile halves and carefully roll to close. Place the stuffed chiles on a baking sheet, seam side down, and transfer to the freezer. Freeze the stuffed chiles for at least 3 hours or overnight.

MAKE THE BATTER: In a stand mixer fitted with the whisk attachment, beat the egg whites until foamy, about 1 minute. Add 1 tablespoon salt and continue beating the whites until nearly stiff, about 3 minutes. Remove the bowl from the stand mixer and carefully fold in the yolks one at a time with a handheld whisk.

Working in batches, gently fold 1¼ cups of flour into the batter. Refrigerate until ready to use (the batter will keep overnight if you want to work ahead).

Meanwhile, place a 5½-quart Dutch oven fitted with a candy thermometer over medium heat and add the vegetable oil, leaving at least 3 inches of space between the surface of the oil and the lip of the pot. Heat until the thermometer registers 350°F.

Make one batch of tortillas and hold them warm.

FRY AND SAUCE THE CHILES: Line a large plate with paper towels and sprinkle the remaining 1 cup flour on a separate plate. Remove the stuffed chiles from the freezer and the batter from the refrigerator. Dredge each chile in the flour and gently shake off any excess. Dip the chiles into the batter one by one and carefully add to the hot oil, working in small batches so as to not crowd them. Fry the chiles until golden brown, about 3 minutes. Transfer to the prepared plate and season with salt.

Set a 12-inch sauté pan over medium heat and warm the Salsa Ranchera until steaming-hot. Add the fried chiles to the sauce and turn to coat evenly. Remove from the heat and set aside in a warm place.

ASSEMBLE THE TACOS: Lay out the warm tortillas on serving plates. Place a chile relleno on each tortilla and top with some of the remaining Salsa Ranchera. Squeeze a couple of the lime wedges over the tacos and serve the rest on the side.

A NOTE ON
BLACK GARLIC

This recipe calls for black garlic—garlic cloves that have been caramelized at a glacial pace until their color deepens, their texture softens, and their flavor mellows and becomes sweet. Black garlic offers a distinctive depth, so it's worth tracking down online or at a specialized grocer. For this recipe, if you can't find black garlic, substitute roasted garlic.

BLACK BEAN HUMMUS TACOS
WITH AYOCOTE BEANS AND AVOCADO

The ancient Aztec diet of beans on tortillas inspired this taco, which packs as much protein as it does compulsive flavor. Black ayocote beans are the backbone of this recipe: the meaty specimens, also called runner beans in the United States, puree into a smooth hummus seasoned with burnt jalapeño ash and salty Cotija cheese. Be warned that one taste of an ayocote is going to ruin chickpeas for you for life. Consider making a double batch of the hummus so you can snack on it for a few days.

MAKES 12 TACOS

ADVANCE PREPARATION

1 recipe Cooked Black Ayocote Beans (page 226)

4 tablespoons Burnt Jalapeño Powder (page 226)

Crema Mexicana (page 233)

FOR THE FILLING

¼ cup extra-virgin olive oil

Kosher salt, as needed

1 jalapeño chile, stemmed and roughly chopped

¼ cup tahini

4 black garlic cloves, peeled

½ cup crumbled Cotija cheese

¼ cup fresh lime juice

TO ASSEMBLE THE TACOS

1 Haas avocado, cut into 24 slices lengthwise

½ cup crumbled Cotija cheese

½ medium white onion, minced

60 cilantro leaves (from about 15 sprigs), roughly chopped

2 limes, each cut into 6 wedges

1 recipe Corn or Flour Tortillas (page 35 or 41)

MAKE THE FILLING: Rinse the Cooked Black Ayocote Beans in a colander under running water. Transfer half of the beans to a large bowl and dress them with 2 tablespoons of the olive oil. Taste the beans and adjust the seasoning with salt. Set aside.

Add the remaining 2 tablespoons olive oil to a large sauté pan and set over medium heat. When the oil is shimmering, add the jalapeño and sweat for 2 minutes. Add the remaining half of the ayocote beans to the pan along with the tahini, Burnt Jalapeño Powder, and black garlic. Stir the mixture and continue cooking until it steams, about 3 minutes.

Remove the bean-tahini mixture from the heat and transfer to a food processor along with ½ cup Cotija cheese and the lime juice. Process until smooth. Taste the hummus and adjust the seasoning with salt.

Make one batch of tortillas and hold them warm.

ASSEMBLE THE TACOS: Lay out the warm tortillas on serving plates. Place a few tablespoons of the hummus on each tortilla and spread using the back of a spoon. Add 2 slices of avocado to each taco, along with some of the dressed ayocote beans and a dollop of Crema Mexicana. Top with the remaining Cotija cheese, minced onion, and chopped cilantro. Squeeze a couple of the lime wedges over the tacos and serve the rest on the side.

MASHED PEA TACOS
WITH PARMESAN CHEESE

Mexico's year-round heat has resulted in a cuisine that seems to defy the seasons, at least from an American northeasterner's perspective. But while all of my restaurants exalt that country's cooking, I'm still compelled to use things like asparagus and ramps when they are available at the market in New York City. Making the most of seasonal produce without losing the soul of Mexican food is the challenge that inspired this taco. The smooth, complex blend of spring peas with olive oil and toasted chiles calls to mind Mexico's tradition of frijoles refritos (refried beans). Aged Mexican cheeses such as Cotija añejo are difficult to find in the United States, so I use Parmesan here to supply the umami funk.

MAKES 12 TACOS

FOR THE FILLING

4 pasilla Oaxaqueño chiles

1½ pounds shelled English peas, blanched (about 5 cups)

1 cup grated Parmesan cheese

¼ cup extra-virgin olive oil

Kosher salt, as needed

TO ASSEMBLE THE TACOS

36 pea tendrils

1 cup grated Parmesan cheese

2 limes, each cut into 6 wedges

1 recipe Corn or Flour Tortillas (page 35 or 41)

MAKE THE FILLING: Set a 12-inch cast-iron skillet over medium heat for 5 minutes. Remove the stems from the pasilla Oaxaqueño chiles and tear the chiles open. Shake out and discard the seeds. Remove and discard the veins.

Toast the chiles in the skillet, turning from time to time, until you see the first wisp of smoke, about 30 seconds. Turn off the heat and transfer 2 of the chiles to a bowl, cover with hot tap water, and submerge them with a plate. Set aside to soak for 30 minutes.

Place the remaining 2 chiles in a spice grinder and grind to a fine powder.

Add the peas and 1 cup grated Parmesan to a food processor and process until smooth.

Drain the soaked chiles, and discard the liquid. Roughly chop the chiles and add them to the pea-Parmesan mixture along with the oil and salt. Process until smooth.

Make one batch of tortillas and hold them warm.

ASSEMBLE THE TACOS: Lay out the warm tortillas on serving plates. Place a few tablespoons of the pea puree on each tortilla and spread using the back of a spoon. Top with the pea tendrils, the remaining 1 cup grated Parmesan, and a sprinkle of the toasted chile powder. Squeeze a couple of the lime wedges over the tacos and serve the rest on the side.

SQUASH BLOSSOM TACOS

Squash blossoms are handled with kid gloves in American restaurants: gently filled with cheese, crisped in lacy batter, or draped like silk scarves on top of rustic pizzas. Not so in Mexico, where the flores de calabaza are treated less like objets d'art and more like, well, food. They are sautéed with no more grandeur than spinach, and hidden inside quesadillas with black galls of huitlacoche. It isn't a graceful end for such an attractive product, but it is delicious. Wilted in garlicky oil, the blooms absorb flavors just like a leafy green, and they reveal their gumption when paired with threads of Oaxacan string cheese and a smoky, assertive salsa.

MAKES 12 TACOS

ADVANCE PREPARATION

Tomatillo-Chipotle Salsa (page 82), substituting the chipotle chiles with 2 pasillas Oaxaqueños, for serving

Crema Mexicana (page 233), for serving

FOR THE FILLING

¼ cup extra-virgin olive oil

12 garlic cloves, minced

1 medium white onion, thinly sliced

Kosher salt, as needed

72 squash blossoms, halved, pistils removed

TO ASSEMBLE THE TACOS

½ pound quesillo (Oaxacan string cheese), pulled into 3-inch strips

2 limes, each cut into 6 wedges

1 recipe Corn or Flour Tortillas (page 35 or 41)

Make one batch of tortillas and hold them warm.

MAKE THE FILLING: Set a 12-inch sauté pan over medium heat and add the olive oil. Once the oil is shimmering, add the garlic and cook until golden brown. Add the onion slices, season with salt, and cook until translucent. Add the squash blossoms and cook until just wilted, about 2 minutes. Remove the pan from the heat, taste the filling, and adjust the seasoning with salt. Set aside in a warm place.

ASSEMBLE THE TACOS: Lay out the warm tortillas on serving plates. Distribute the squash blossom mixture and the shredded quesillo evenly among the tortillas. Top with some of the Tomatillo-Pasilla Oaxaqueño Salsa and the Crema Mexicana. Squeeze a couple of the lime wedges over the tacos and serve the rest on the side.

ON MEXICO'S

JOLIE LAIDE

The expression *jolie laide* is a compliment so backward that only the French could have devised it. *Jolie laide* means "beautiful ugly" and it's used to describe unconventional beauty, the sort possessed by Charlotte Gainsbourg or Tilda Swinton—or morel mushrooms or geoduck clams. It's an idea that comes into play when I cook Mexican food.

I'm a habitual aesthete when it comes to cooking and plating. I believe that food should look as exquisite as it tastes: meticulous arrangements of herbs, splatters of squid ink, brushstrokes of Mole Poblano, masa piped into loopy wires. It's what I did at Alinea and at wd~50; and I do these things at Empellón because making food look beautiful is part of my creative coding. And maybe a little bit, too, I do this because a dark part of me thinks that inner beauty is a tough sell in a restaurant landscape like New York.

It's a matter of framing, really. When people eat at a taqueria or a street vendor in Mexico, they regard the food differently than they would at a high-end restaurant back home. They give it a wider berth, they allow it to be rustic, unfussy, even messy. I'd love to be able to replicate a traditional dish and present it in a simple way, but outside the bubble of a vacation—far from the native environment that seemed so charming and exotic over Christmas break—guests don't seem to want humble-looking Mexican food. Which is to say that if I let Empellón's food look the way a lot of true Mexican food looks, I'm just not sure people would give it a chance to dazzle them.

I think about this because Mexican food often isn't pretty, at least in the way we've come to define beauty in this fiefdom of haute cuisine. Mexican food is black, brown, and beige. It's saucy food—cooked-within-an-inch-of-its-life food. If you've learned to make fried eggs in a Euro-centric culinary school, for example, you might look at any bit of browning as a failure. But then you eat eggs in Mexico; that's a high-temperature cooking culture where eggs should sizzle when they hit the hot comal, and they are finished when the whites develop dark lacy edges. They're pretty tasty like that, too. Likewise, you might have a Pavlovian response when you see the rare, rosy core of a thick steak. But muscular Mexican beef requires a different kind of handling—it's cooked hard, fast, and often all the way through, because that's what the nature of the ingredient demands. We like stylized food, accessorized plates, camera-ready cuisine. But in Mexico, food, first and foremost, is a thing to be eaten, not beheld.

Then I consider mole. I think of the stack of ingredients required to make it, and of the way its murky color speaks to how each component is conditioned to wring out every lingering molecule of flavor. Or, I think about poblano chiles—how perfectly lovely they look when raw and how much abuse it takes to make them taste their best: they are scorched, then steamed until they lose their vibrant color and give up their wrinkly skin; they are sliced into dull and flaccid strips and suffocated with cream. Poblano *rajas* are busted, man, but they taste like grass and fire and sweetness. They are one of the most delicious things on earth.

In the Mexican kitchen, doing what's best for an ingredient can sometimes mean destroying its raw, natural allure. It might seem counterintuitive to burn chiles to cinder or to cook a puree so aggressively that it explodes in angry splatters. But the more you work with this food, the more you will see the brilliant logic behind this treatment— the flavor that develops when you push beyond what feels natural or safe to most American cooks. You start to see the beauty in the doing.

The truth is, I don't always know how to reconcile my cooking instincts with a cuisine that values flavor over form. I slap my own wrist when I get in the way of this food, because I know that too much fuss will degrade it. Other times, I let myself play because my role is not archivist of Mexican food; I'm a chef with my own identity and the free will to throw myself into something that inspires me. Still, in the case of the Squash Blossom Tacos (page 199) and the Huitlacoche Tacos (page 202), I know where I stand. These tacos might seem homely at first, because in Mexican culture the way they *eat* is a higher priority than the way they *look*. But there is beauty in there, too.

There is jolie laide.

HUITLACOCHE TACOS
WITH SALSA MEXICANA

Huitlacoche is a fungus that transforms normal corn kernels into gray, gnarly blisters that look like the petrified spawn of a cryptid and taste like the rarest, most delicious mushroom foraged from the floor of some dark, accursed forest. I like the entire idea of it. I like how it is considered a blight in this country and a delicacy in Mexico. I like that it looks deformed—I even have a tattoo of warped huitlacoche snaking up my rib cage.

The stuff is fun to work with, but it's impossible to make look pretty. So for this taco I don't even try. I sauté some Salsa Mexicana, then stir in the huitlacoche until it releases its black liquor, heap that stew onto a tortilla with some crema, and let the musky, earthy product speak for itself.

MAKES 12 TACOS

ADVANCE PREPARATION

1 cup Salsa Mexicana (page 70), plus more for serving

Crema Mexicana (page 233), for serving

FOR THE FILLING

2 tablespoons lard or vegetable oil

1¾ pounds huitlacoche (four 7-ounce cans; see Note)

Kosher salt, as needed

TO ASSEMBLE THE TACOS

2 limes, each cut into 6 wedges

1 recipe Corn or Flour Tortillas (page 35 or 41)

MAKE THE FILLING: Set a 12-inch sauté pan over medium heat and add the lard. Once the fat is shimmering, add 1 cup of the Salsa Mexicana and cook until the salsa vegetables are tender and the liquid has reduced by half, about 7 minutes.

Add the huitlacoche to the pan and season with salt. Cook until most of the huitlacoche liquor has evaporated, about 7 minutes. Set aside in a warm place.

Make one batch of tortillas and hold them warm.

ASSEMBLE THE TACOS: Lay out the warm tortillas on serving plates. Distribute the huitlacoche mixture evenly among the tortillas and top with the remaining raw Salsa Mexicana and the Crema Mexicana. Squeeze a couple of the lime wedges over the tacos and serve the rest on the side.

A NOTE ON
HUITLACOCHE

Huitlacoche is cultivated in Mexico, but it's almost impossible to find fresh in the United States. Frozen huitlacoche is available (thaw before use), but you're most likely to find it canned or jarred in a Mexican grocery store. Look for brands like Adelita, Herdez, and Goya; note that it is sometimes spelled *cuitlacoche*, a holdover from the word's Nahuatl roots. Make sure to drain and rinse the brine if you're using canned or jarred huitlacoche.

CARROT TACOS
WITH ARGAN OIL MOLE

I first tasted carrots seasoned with argan oil while working at Clío in Boston, and I couldn't get over the combination. The mix of earthy root vegetable and nutty aromatic oil stayed with me for years. But to pull that flavor into a Mexican context at Empellón, I had to do some free association. Argan oil comes from the nut of the Moroccan argan tree, and nuts, of course, are a fundamental part of traditional moles. The mole used in this recipe is built on that thought, with almonds and sesame seeds, fried chiles, and dried fruits like apricots and prunes in deference to argan's North African origin. The deep, rich, slow-cooked flavor of the sauce plays against the sweetness of roasted carrots and the tanginess of crumbled goat cheese.

MAKES 12 TACOS

ADVANCE PREPARATION

2½ cups Argan Oil Mole (page 95)

FOR THE FILLING

1 cup panko bread crumbs

3 tablespoons argan oil

2 teaspoons kosher salt, plus more as needed

50 baby carrots (see Note, page 204), scrubbed and stemmed

1 cup cider vinegar

1 tablespoon packed dark brown sugar

20 black peppercorns

½ medium white onion, thinly sliced

8 tablespoons (1 stick) unsalted butter

TO ASSEMBLE THE TACOS

6 ounces goat cheese, crumbled

1 cup loosely packed watercress leaves

1 recipe Corn or Flour Tortillas (page 35 or 41)

BEGIN THE FILLING: In a small bowl, mix the bread crumbs, argan oil, and 1 teaspoon salt.

Line a plate with paper towels. Set an 8-inch sauté pan over medium heat and add the bread-crumb mixture. Toast until the bread crumbs are slightly golden, about 2 minutes, shaking the pan to prevent burning. Remove from the heat and transfer the bread crumbs to the prepared plate.

Slice 2 of the baby carrots into very thin rounds and place in a small, nonreactive bowl. Set a 1-quart saucepan over medium heat and add the vinegar, brown sugar, 1 teaspoon salt, the peppercorns, and onion slices. Bring to a simmer, then remove from the heat and pour over the sliced carrots. Let the pickled carrots steep until ready to use.

recipe continues

Line a baking sheet with paper towels. Set a 12-inch sauté pan over medium heat and add 4 tablespoons of the butter. Whisk continuously until the butter turns a light brown, about 3½ minutes. Add half of the remaining baby carrots to the pan, lower the heat, and cook, shaking the pan from time to time, until the carrots are lightly caramelized and tender, 20 to 25 minutes. Remove the carrots from the heat and transfer to the prepared baking sheet. Season with salt.

Clean the sauté pan and set back over medium heat. Add the remaining 4 tablespoons butter and repeat the cooking process with the remaining baby carrots.

Make one batch of tortillas and hold them warm.

FINISH THE FILLING: Clean the sauté pan and set back over medium heat. Add 1¼ cups of the Argan Oil Mole and heat until warm. Add half of the cooked baby carrots to glaze them. Remove from the pan and transfer to a plate. Repeat the process with another 1¼ cups of Argan Oil Mole and the remaining baby carrots.

ASSEMBLE THE TACOS: Lay out the warm tortillas on serving plates. Evenly distribute the cooked baby carrots among the tortillas and drizzle with some of the remaining Argan Oil Mole from the pan. Top with the pickled carrots, the crumbled goat cheese and watercress leaves, and a sprinkle of the toasted bread crumbs.

A NOTE ON
BABY CARROTS

When I talk about baby carrots in this recipe I am not talking about those little peeled nubs rotting in a cellophane bag, waiting for someone to come along and dip them in ranch dressing. Instead, I mean immature carrots that are sweet, tender, and quick-cooking. They come in bunches with green tops, just like full-size carrots. The peel is thin enough that it does not need to be removed—just wash, scrub, slice off the tops, and leave their tips intact.

RAW PORCINI MUSHROOM TACOS
WITH SAVORY ARROZ CON LECHE

In the Stupak household of the 1980s, the tradition of the economical casserole was alive and well. My mom wasn't the cook in my family, but she had a few grand slams in her culinary Rolodex. Her combination of rice baked with hammered pork chops and cream of mushroom soup was a perennial favorite. This taco is inspired by my memories of that casserole—fond ones, in spite of everything I've learned as a chef since. Here, I cook rice in brown butter and milk steeped with canela, epazote, and chipotle until it's sticky and thick. Folding the gachas (Spanish for "porridge") into lightly whipped cream loosens its texture, and a hit of fish sauce plays up the raw-mushroom umami.

MAKES 12 TACOS

ADVANCE PREPARATION

Tomatillo-Chipotle Salsa (page 82), for serving

FOR THE FILLING

Two 2-inch sticks of canela (Mexican cinnamon)

1 pasilla chile

1 chipotle morita chile

1 epazote branch

4 tablespoons (½ stick) unsalted butter

2 shallots, minced

½ cup medium-grain rice

¼ cup dry sherry

Kosher salt, as needed

2 cups milk

1 cup heavy cream

1 tablespoon fish sauce

6 fresh porcini mushrooms, cleaned and sliced thin on a mandoline

TO ASSEMBLE THE TACOS

½ medium white onion, minced

2 limes, each cut into 6 wedges

1 recipe Corn or Flour Tortillas (page 35 or 41)

EQUIPMENT: cheesecloth, butcher's twine, mandoline slicer

MAKE THE FILLING: Set a 12-inch cast-iron skillet over medium heat for 5 minutes. Add 1 stick of canela and toast briefly, shaking the pan, until fragrant, about 15 seconds. Remove from the heat, transfer to a spice grinder, and grind to a fine powder. Transfer to a bowl.

Remove the stem from the pasilla chile and tear the chile open. Shake out the seeds, and remove and discard the veins.

In the skillet, toast the pasilla chile, turning from time to time,

until you see the first wisp of smoke, about 30 seconds. Remove from the heat, transfer the chile to a spice grinder, and grind to a fine powder. Transfer to a bowl.

Cut a 6-inch square of cheesecloth. In the center, place the chipotle morita chile, the remaining stick of canela, and the epazote branch. Roll into a sachet and tie with twine.

Set a 4-quart saucepan over medium heat and add the butter. Whisk continuously until it turns a light brown, about 3 minutes. Add the shallots and sweat, about 3 minutes. Add the rice and stir to evenly coat with the brown butter. Pour in the sherry and cook until the alcohol evaporates, about 1 minute. Add 2 cups water, followed by the sachet, and then season with salt. Bring the mixture to a simmer and lower the heat to maintain the simmer. Stir occasionally. Cook uncovered until the water is absorbed by the rice, about 15 minutes.

Add the milk and continue to simmer, stirring constantly until the milk is absorbed and the mixture is thick, about 15 minutes. Season with salt. Remove from the heat, spread the rice in a shallow pan or baking tray, and place in the refrigerator to cool for 20 minutes.

In a bowl, whip the cream to soft peaks and fold in the fish sauce. Remove the cooled rice mixture from the refrigerator and gently combine it with the whipped cream.

Make one batch of tortillas and hold them warm.

ASSEMBLE THE TACOS: Lay out the warm tortillas on serving plates. Distribute the arroz con leche evenly among the tortillas and drizzle with some Tomatillo-Chipotle Salsa. Arrange a thin layer of porcini slices on top and sprinkle with the minced onion, ground canela, and ground pasilla. Squeeze a couple of the lime wedges over the tacos and serve the rest on the side.

MIXED MUSHROOM TACOS
WITH EPAZOTE PESTO

Similar to mint and peas or basil and tomatoes, epazote and mushrooms is a reflex pairing in Mexico. But unlike those herbs, epazote isn't often eaten raw. To tame its pungent, almost petroleum-like flavor for this recipe, we infuse the epazote in a kind of Mexican pesto, made with walnuts instead of pine nuts and Cotija cheese instead of Parmesan. The pesto adds a ton of dimension when drizzled over mushrooms cooked down in chile puree and folded into a simple, vegetarian-friendly taco. Just about any mushroom will work here, although portobellos don't hold up as well.

MAKES 12 TACOS

FOR THE EPAZOTE PESTO

1 cup extra-virgin olive oil

½ cup raw walnuts, roughly chopped

6 garlic cloves, peeled

60 epazote leaves (from about 10 branches), roughly chopped

3 tablespoons crumbled Cotija cheese

Kosher salt, as needed

FOR THE FILLING

5 pasilla Oaxaqueño chiles

5 garlic cloves, skins on

3 tablespoons lard or vegetable oil

2 pounds mixed mushrooms, such as maitake or shiitake, roughly chopped

1 teaspoon kosher salt

TO ASSEMBLE THE TACOS

2 limes, each cut into 6 wedges

1 recipe Corn or Flour Tortillas (page 35 or 41)

MAKE THE EPAZOTE PESTO: Set a 12-inch sauté pan over medium heat and add the olive oil. Once the oil is shimmering, add the walnuts and garlic cloves, and cook until golden brown, about 3 minutes. Remove the pan from the heat and add the chopped epazote. Transfer the mixture to a bowl and set into an ice bath to cool.

In a food processor, combine the walnut-epazote mixture and the Cotija cheese. Process the mixture to a coarse puree. Taste and adjust seasoning with salt. Transfer to a bowl.

MAKE THE FILLING: Remove the stems from the pasilla Oaxaqueño chiles and tear the chiles open. Shake out and discard the seeds. Remove and discard the veins.

Set a 12-inch cast-iron skillet over medium heat for 5 minutes. Add the chiles and toast, turning them from time to time, until you see the first wisp of smoke, about 30 seconds. Transfer the chiles to a bowl, cover with hot tap water,

and place a heavy plate over the chiles to keep them submerged. Set aside to soak for 30 minutes.

Reheat the skillet over medium heat. Add the garlic cloves and roast, turning them from time to time, until softened slightly and blackened in spots, about 6 minutes. Turn off the heat, remove the garlic from the skillet, and set aside to cool at room temperature. Once they are cool enough to handle, peel the garlic cloves and discard the skins.

Drain the soaked chiles, and discard the liquid. Place the chiles in a blender along with the roasted garlic and 2 cups of fresh water, and puree on high speed until completely smooth.

Set a 6-quart stockpot over medium heat and add the lard. Once the fat is smoking, pour in the puree all at once; it will sputter. Lower the heat to a simmer and stir the puree with a wooden spoon as it cooks down to a thick, dark paste, about 15 minutes.

Add the mushrooms to the stock-pot and season with salt. Cook until tender, about 5 minutes, then set aside in a warm place.

Make one batch of tortillas and hold them warm.

ASSEMBLE THE TACOS: Lay out the warm tortillas on serving plates. Distribute the mixed mushrooms evenly among the tortillas and top with some of the epazote pesto. Squeeze a couple of the lime wedges over the tacos and serve the rest on the side.

WILD SPINACH TACOS
WITH PINE NUT SALSA

Wild spinach, also known as lamb's quarters in the United States and as quelites in Mexico, is a fascinating green. The spiky, diamond-shaped leaves grow like weeds—you can even spot them in New York City parks—and are available in farmers' markets throughout the summer. Unlike conventional spinach, lamb's quarters don't release all of their water when heated, so they stand up well to a sauté and offer a gratifying texture with plenty of chew. The greens are almost aggressively healthful, so we let them stay that way in this taco, adding some gentle chipotle heat and modest richness: just a crumble of queso fresco, pine nut salsa, and a sprinkle of pine nuts boiled to bring out their beanlike creaminess.

MAKES 12 TACOS

ADVANCE PREPARATION

Pine Nut Salsa (page 92), for serving

FOR THE FILLING

¾ cup pine nuts

Kosher salt, as needed

¼ cup extra-virgin olive oil

6 garlic cloves, thinly sliced

4 canned chipotle chiles, minced

2 bunches wild spinach (lamb's quarters), leaves only (4 packed cups)

Freshly ground black pepper, as needed

TO ASSEMBLE THE TACOS

1 cup crumbled queso fresco

2 limes, each cut into 6 wedges

1 recipe Corn or Flour Tortillas (page 35 or 41)

MAKE THE FILLING: Set an 8-inch sauté pan over medium heat for 5 minutes. Add the pine nuts and toast until golden, shaking the pan frequently to prevent them from burning, about 45 seconds. Add 2 cups water, bring to a boil, then lower the heat to a simmer. Season with salt and simmer for another 5 minutes, or until the pine nuts are slightly softened with some bite. Remove the pan from the heat, strain the pine nuts, and set aside.

Set a 12-inch sauté pan over medium heat and add the olive oil. When the oil is shimmering, add the garlic and cook until golden brown. Add the chipotle chiles and stir to combine.

Gently fold the wild spinach into the garlic-chipotle mixture. Season to taste with salt and black pepper. Cook the spinach until just wilted, about 2 minutes. Remove the pan from the heat and set aside in a warm place.

Make one batch of tortillas and hold them warm.

ASSEMBLE THE TACOS: Lay out the warm tortillas on serving plates. Evenly distribute the spinach mixture among the tortillas and drizzle with the Pine Nut Salsa. Top with the boiled pine nuts and crumbled queso fresco. Squeeze a couple of the lime wedges over the tacos and serve the rest on the side.

DEVILED EGG TACOS
WITH SIKIL PAK

It's peculiar that hard-boiled eggs are such a crucial part of Yucatecan cooking; you don't see much of them elsewhere in Mexican cuisine. But boiled eggs are everywhere throughout the peninsula: stuffed into tamales, rolled into enchilada-like papadzules, stewed with ground meat and chile paste in relleno negro—the list goes on. This taco is a nod to that tradition. We devil the yolks with salsa habanera and pair the halved eggs with red onion and sikil pak, a pumpkin seed dip common in the Yucatán. The taco is spicy and nutty, with the satisfying texture of firm whites and creamy yolks bundled in a supple tortilla.

MAKES 12 TACOS

ADVANCE PREPARATION

½ teaspoon Salsa Habanera (page 62), plus more for serving

¾ cup Sikil Pak (page 91)

FOR THE FILLING

12 hard-boiled eggs, peeled

1 tablespoon Dijon mustard

2 tablespoons mayonnaise

Kosher salt, as needed

TO ASSEMBLE THE TACOS

½ medium red onion, minced

60 cilantro leaves (from about 15 sprigs), roughly chopped

2 limes, each cut into 6 wedges

1 recipe Corn or Flour Tortillas (page 35 or 41)

MAKE THE FILLING. Slice each egg in half lengthwise. Carefully scoop out the yolks and transfer to a large bowl. Set the whites aside on a plate.

Add the Dijon mustard, mayonnaise, and ½ teaspoon of the Salsa Habanera to the yolks and whisk together until smooth. Taste and adjust the seasoning with salt.

Spoon the yolk mixture into a pastry bag fitted with a star tip. Pipe a rosette of the mixture into each cavity of the egg whites. Set the deviled eggs aside at room temperature until ready to serve.

Make one batch of tortillas and hold them warm.

ASSEMBLE THE TACOS: Lay out the warm tortillas on serving plates. Place a tablespoon of Sikil Pak on each tortilla and spread using the back of a spoon. Evenly distribute the deviled eggs among the tortillas and top with the minced onion, chopped cilantro, and a small amount of Salsa Habanera. Squeeze a couple of the lime wedges over the tacos and serve the rest on the side.

BREAKFAST TACOS
WITH SALSA DE ÁRBOL

Texas food authority Robb Walsh describes Tex-Mex as an American regional cuisine evolved from native Tejano cooking and the spicing traditions of eighteenth-century immigrants from the Canary Islands. There's a lot to consider there for an essentialist like me. That Tex-Mex is not an extrapolation of Mexican food but, rather, its own established tradition, influenced as much by geography, colonization, and migration patterns as Mexico itself. That foods like queso, chile con carne, and fajitas are actually totemic American-regional dishes with their own, independent measures of authenticity. I haven't explored Tex-Mex much in my restaurants, and frankly I don't think the cuisine needs another champion. Texas has done such a good job in exporting this food to the rest of the country that the lines separating it from Mexican traditions have blurred, and most Americans don't distinguish between the two. Still, there's one foodstuff that the Lone Star State has kept mostly to itself; it's time to reconsider the breakfast taco.

The specific contents of a breakfast taco vary, but eggs, chorizo, potato, and cheese are common. For this nod to the pride of Austin, I fold Chihuahua cheese, red chorizo, and crumbled potato chips into soft scrambled eggs and top it with my kind of hot sauce: salsa de árbol.

MAKES 12 TACOS

ADVANCE PREPARATION

1 cup Red Chorizo (page 228)

Salsa de Árbol (page 65), for serving

Crema Mexicana (page 233), for serving

FOR THE FILLING

One 8-ounce bag kettle-cooked potato chips

2 tablespoons lard or vegetable oil

12 large eggs, lightly beaten

1 cup grated Chihuahua cheese

TO ASSEMBLE THE TACOS

½ medium white onion, minced

60 cilantro leaves (from about 15 sprigs), roughly chopped

2 limes, each cut into 6 wedges

1 recipe Corn or Flour Tortillas (page 35 or 41)

BEGIN THE FILLING: In a bowl, lightly crumble the potato chips with your hands and set aside.

Set a 3½-quart Dutch oven over medium heat and add 1 tablespoon of the lard. Once the fat is shimmering, add the Red Chorizo and cook until it is crumbly and has completely rendered its fat. Remove from the heat and transfer to a bowl.

Make one batch of tortillas and hold them warm.

FINISH THE FILLING: Add the remaining tablespoon of lard to the Dutch oven and set back over medium heat. Once the fat is shimmering, add the eggs and whisk continuously. As soon as the eggs are soft and creamy, remove from the heat. Fold in the Chihuahua cheese, cooked chorizo, and half the crumbled potato chips, reserving the rest for garnish.

ASSEMBLE THE TACOS: Lay out the warm tortillas on serving plates. Distribute the scrambled eggs evenly among the tortillas. Top with the remaining crumbled potato chips, a drizzle of Salsa de Árbol and Crema Mexicana, and the minced onion and chopped cilantro. Squeeze a couple of the lime wedges over the tacos and serve the rest on the side.

SUNNYSIDE DUCK EGG TACOS
WITH GREEN CHORIZO GRAVY

Rust-colored, dried chile chorizo is fairly common in the States, but its bright-green cousin has yet to get much attention here. Green chorizo is the centerpiece of this egg-and-gravy breakfast taco: crumbly pork tinted with parsley and fresh green chiles, thickened with cream and masa. The fried duck eggs hold their vibrant, sturdy yolks longer than chicken eggs, but they will still gush out the sides when you fold this taco and take a bite—napkins are vital.

MAKES 12 TACOS

ADVANCE PREPARATION

1 recipe Green Chorizo (page 227)

FOR THE GREEN CHORIZO GRAVY

2 medium tomatillos (about 3 ounces total), husked, rinsed, and patted dry

2 cups heavy cream

1 tablespoon masa harina

1 tablespoon whole-grain mustard

FOR THE FILLING

4 tablespoons (½ stick) unsalted butter

12 duck eggs

Kosher salt and freshly ground black pepper, as needed

TO ASSEMBLE THE TACOS

½ medium white onion, minced

60 cilantro leaves (from about 15 sprigs), roughly chopped

2 limes, each cut into 6 wedges

1 recipe Corn or Flour Tortillas (page 35 or 41)

MAKE THE GREEN CHORIZO GRAVY: Preheat the broiler. Roast the tomatillos on a baking sheet until blackened in spots, about 7 minutes. Turn them over and continue to blacken, another 7 minutes. Remove from the broiler and set aside to cool to room temperature. Transfer to a blender.

Set a 1-quart saucepan over medium heat and add the cream. Bring to a simmer, then immediately remove from the heat and transfer to the blender with the roasted tomatillos. Add the masa harina and mustard, and puree on high speed until completely smooth.

Set a 4-quart saucepan over medium heat for 5 minutes. Add the Green Chorizo and cook until crumbly, about 5 minutes. Pour in the cream-tomatillo mixture and bring to a simmer. Cook until slightly thickened, about 5 minutes. Remove the pan from the heat; set aside in a warm place.

Make one batch of tortillas and hold them warm.

MAKE THE FILLING: Set a 12-inch nonstick skillet over medium heat and melt 1 tablespoon of the butter. Once the butter sizzles, crack 3 eggs into the skillet and season with salt and black pepper. Cook the eggs until the whites are completely set, 3 to 5 minutes. Carefully transfer to a plate and set aside in a warm place.

Repeat the process three more times with the remaining butter and duck eggs.

ASSEMBLE THE TACOS: Lay out the warm tortillas on serving plates. Place an egg on each tortilla and top with the gravy, the minced onion, and the chopped cilantro. Squeeze a couple of the lime wedges over the tacos and serve the rest on the side.

NATAS TACOS
WITH PICKLED STRAWBERRIES

In England, the buttery skin that's peeled from the surface of scalding milk is fundamental to a classic Devonshire tea service. They call it clotted cream and smear it on scones with jam. In the dairy-producing regions of Mexico, the same stuff is called natas, and it's eaten in a similar way: heaped with fruit preserves on squishy rolls. This breakfasty taco captures that combination of rich dairy and sweet fruit with heaps of natas, pickled strawberries, brown butter, and sprigs of lemony herbs.

If you can't find raw milk to make the natas, try this taco with store-bought clotted cream, or even a great ricotta cheese.

MAKES 12 TACOS

ADVANCE PREPARATION

1 recipe Natas (page 233)

FOR THE FILLING

24 ripe strawberries, hulled

1 tablespoon extra-virgin olive oil

1 shallot, thinly sliced

2 cups cider vinegar

¼ cup packed dark brown sugar

½ tablespoon kosher salt

2 tablespoons unsalted butter

TO ASSEMBLE THE TACOS

Maldon or flaky salt, as needed

1 tablespoon freshly ground black pepper

36 sprigs of lemon balm or mint

1 recipe Corn or Flour Tortillas (page 35 or 41)

MAKE THE FILLING: Place the strawberries in a large, nonreactive bowl. Set a 1-quart saucepan over medium heat and add the olive oil. Once the oil is shimmering, add the shallot and cook until translucent. Add the vinegar, brown sugar, and salt. Bring to a simmer, then immediately remove from the heat and pour over the strawberries. Steep for about 10 minutes.

Set an 8-inch sauté pan over medium heat and add the butter. Whisk continuously until it turns a light brown, about 2½ minutes.

Line a plate with paper towels. Drain the strawberries and discard the pickling liquid. Transfer the berries to the prepared plate. Slice the strawberries in half.

Make one batch of tortillas and hold them warm.

ASSEMBLE THE TACOS: Lay out the warm tortillas on serving plates. Place a few tablespoons of Natas on each tortilla and spread with the back of a spoon. Distribute the pickled strawberries evenly among the tortillas and top with the brown butter. Sprinkle with the Maldon salt, black pepper, and a few sprigs of lemon balm or mint.

CHOCOLATE TACOS

It's impossible to talk about Mexican cuisine without considering the influence of Spain. Foods that are fundamental to the culture—things like rice and pork—got to Mexico in the hulls of sixteenth-century conquistador ships. As a cook, I find it interesting to continue to mash up culinary concepts from both countries, even if they aren't the result of centuries of colonization and indigenous fusion. For this sweet taco, I co-opted pan con chocolate, a common after-school snack in Spain: It's simply a piece of lush couverture (I like Mast Brothers, produced here in New York City) melted on a tortilla instead of toast, with sea salt, chile powder, and cinnamon to evoke the spiced flavor of Mexican chocolate. Call it a Choco Taco, if you absolutely must.

MAKES 12 TACOS

FOR THE FILLING

1 pasilla chile

One 2-inch stick of canela (Mexican cinnamon)

8 ounces dark chocolate

TO ASSEMBLE THE TACOS

2 tablespoons extra-virgin olive oil

Maldon or flaky salt, as needed

1 recipe Corn or Flour Tortillas (page 35 or 41)

MAKE THE FILLING: Remove the stem from the pasilla chile and tear the chile open. Shake out the seeds, and remove and discard the veins.

Set a 12-inch cast-iron skillet over medium heat for 5 minutes. Add the chile and toast, turning it from time to time, until you see the first wisp of smoke, about 30 seconds. Remove from the heat, transfer to a spice grinder, and grind to a fine powder. Transfer to a bowl.

Reheat the skillet over medium heat. Toast the canela briefly, shaking the pan, until fragrant, about 15 seconds. Remove the canela from the heat, transfer it to the spice grinder, and grind it to a fine powder.

Break the chocolate into rough 1-inch pieces.

Make one batch of tortillas and hold them warm.

ASSEMBLE THE TACOS: Lay out the warm tortillas on serving plates. Immediately divide the broken chocolate among the tortillas and top with the olive oil. Season with Maldon salt and finish with the ground chile and canela.

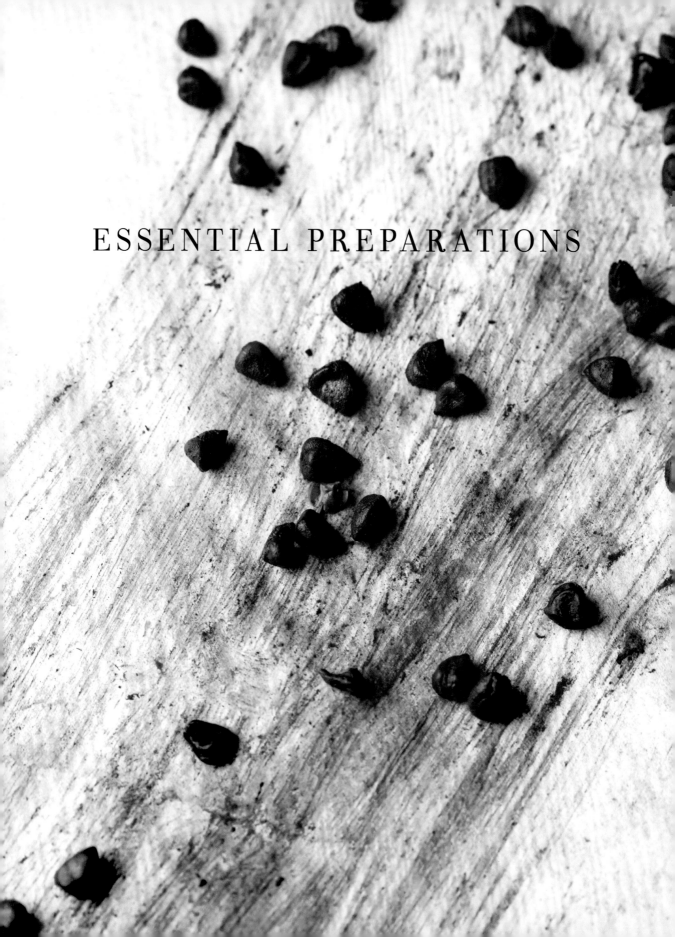

ESSENTIAL PREPARATIONS

ADOBO

Masa may be the bedrock of Mexican cuisine, but adobo is what makes it sing. The dried chile paste is a component in countless dishes, slathered on robust meats like the pork for Al Pastor Tacos (page 130) and the lamb for the Lamb Barbacoa Tacos (page 152). The dried chile and aromatic spice flavors in this paste are versatile, so adobo is a useful thing to have around to add instant depth—try thinning it with oil and using it to dress a hearty vegetable, like asparagus. Adobo will last 1 week in the refrigerator, and 1 month in an airtight container in the freezer.

MAKES ABOUT 2⅓ CUPS

8 ancho chiles

8 guajillo chiles

1 chipotle morita chile

3 whole cloves

¼ teaspoon cumin seeds

One 2-inch stick of canela (Mexican cinnamon)

1 teaspoon black peppercorns

1 teaspoon dried Mexican oregano

20 garlic cloves, skins on

1 cup cider vinegar

Remove the stems from the chiles and tear the chiles open. Shake out and discard the seeds. Tear the chiles into small pieces.

Set a 12-inch cast-iron skillet over medium heat for 5 minutes. Add the cloves, cumin seeds, canela, black peppercorns, and oregano; toast, shaking the pan, until fragrant, about 15 seconds. Remove the spices from the heat, transfer to a spice grinder, and grind to a fine powder.

Reheat the skillet over medium heat. Toast the ancho, guajillo, and chipotle morita chiles, turning from time to time until you see the first wisp of smoke, about 30 seconds. Transfer the chiles to a bowl, cover with hot tap water, and place a heavy plate over the chiles to keep them submerged. Set aside to soak for 30 minutes.

Add the garlic cloves to the skillet and roast, turning them from time to time, until softened slightly and blackened in spots, about 6 minutes. Turn off the heat, remove the garlic from the skillet, and set aside to cool at room temperature. Once the cloves are cool enough to handle, peel them and discard the skins.

Drain the chiles and place in a blender along with the ground spices, roasted garlic, and vinegar, and puree to a paste. You may need to add a bit of water to the blender to help the chiles pass easily through the blades. Transfer to a container and refrigerate until ready to use.

ACHIOTE PASTE

Also called *annatto*, the strange nubby seeds that constitute this seasoning paste are harvested from the spiny fruits of tropical achiote shrubs. Achiote is used as food coloring in many parts of the world (notice how your hands turn orange as you work with it). But the seeds are part of a staple spice rub in Mexican cookery, especially in Oaxaca and the Yucatán. Achiote is slightly bitter and medicinal, but those flavors mellow out when combined with garlic and the wintery notes of cinnamon and allspice in this paste. I slather it on Cochinita Pibil Tacos (page 141), but you could use it to season chicken or grilled shrimp or add it to the water when cooking rice. Achiote paste will last up to 1 month in an airtight container in the refrigerator.

MAKES ABOUT 1¾ CUPS

One 4-inch stick of canela (Mexican cinnamon)

2 tablespoons black peppercorns

2 tablespoons allspice berries

3 tablespoons dried Mexican oregano

½ cup achiote seeds

40 garlic cloves, skins on

1¼ cups cider vinegar

Set a 12-inch cast-iron skillet over medium heat for 5 minutes. Add the canela, black peppercorns, allspice berries, oregano, and achiote seeds; toast, shaking the pan, until fragrant, about 15 seconds. Remove from the heat, transfer to a spice grinder, and grind to a fine powder, working in batches if necessary.

Reheat the skillet over medium heat. Add the garlic cloves and roast, turning them from time to time, until softened slightly and blackened in spots, about 6 minutes. Turn off the heat, remove the garlic from the skillet, and set aside to cool at room temperature. Once they are cool enough to handle, peel the garlic cloves and discard the skins.

In a blender, combine the ground spices and seeds, roasted garlic, and the cider vinegar, and puree until smooth. Transfer to a container and refrigerate until ready to use.

MOJO DE AJO

This tasty Veracruz garlic oil is a handy thing to have around to dress seafood, meat, and vegetables. If you cook the garlic and tomatoes thoroughly, you can safely store it in the refrigerator in an airtight container for up to 1 month.

MAKES ABOUT 1⅔ CUPS

2 árbol chiles

½ teaspoon black peppercorns

½ teaspoon dried Mexican oregano

1 cup extra-virgin olive oil

20 garlic cloves, minced

Juice of 1 orange

1 plum tomato, diced

Remove the stems from the árbol chiles and gently roll the chiles between your fingers to remove the seeds. Discard the seeds.

Set a 12-inch cast-iron skillet over medium heat for 5 minutes. Add the black peppercorns, oregano, and chiles; toast, shaking the pan, until fragrant, about 15 seconds. Remove from the heat, transfer to a spice grinder, and grind to a fine powder.

Set a 1-quart saucepot over medium heat and add the olive oil and garlic. Cook until the garlic begins to turn golden brown, stirring often to prevent it from sticking to the pan. Add the orange juice and tomato, followed by the ground spices and stir to combine. Continue to cook until the tomato has softened, about 2 minutes.

Remove the mixture from the heat and let cool to room temperature. Transfer to a container and refrigerate until ready to use.

CHILMOLE

I've heard tales that the Aztecs used to fit their arrows with smoldering chiles to smoke out enemies during battle. It's an easy enough thing to imagine when you're preparing *chilmole*, an ancient chile-spice compound made by incinerating dried árbols and anchos. While the chiles are burning, turn off your smoke alarm, open the windows and doors, and do your best to hold your breath. You'll sacrifice air quality to make this stuff, but you'll be rewarded with one of the most unique ingredients in the Mexican pantry. Finished chilmole tastes of smoke and char; it's herbal and garlicky, with a soft, lingering heat from the burnt chiles. A single batch goes a long way, and it will keep for up to 3 months in the refrigerator.

MAKES ABOUT 2¾ CUPS

1½ teaspoons allspice berries

1½ teaspoons black peppercorns

1½ teaspoons dried Mexican oregano

1 teaspoon whole cloves

10 garlic cloves, skins on

100 árbol chiles, stemmed

8 ancho chiles, stemmed

1 tablespoon cider vinegar

1 tablespoon kosher salt

Set a 12-inch cast-iron skillet over medium heat for 5 minutes. Add the allspice berries, black peppercorns, oregano, and cloves; toast, shaking the pan, until fragrant, about 15 seconds. Remove from the heat, transfer to a spice grinder, and grind to a fine powder.

Reheat the skillet over medium heat. Add the garlic cloves and roast, turning them from time to time, until softened slightly and blackened in spots, about 6 minutes. Turn off the heat, remove the garlic from the skillet, and set aside to cool at room temperature. Once they are cool enough to handle, peel the garlic cloves and discard the skins.

Preheat the broiler. Place the árbol and ancho chiles on separate baking sheets. Roast the chiles under the broiler until uniformly black and brittle, but not to ashes, about 3 minutes. Transfer the chiles to a bowl, cover with hot tap water, and place a heavy plate over the chiles to keep them submerged. Set aside to soak for 30 minutes.

Drain the chiles and rinse under cold water until it runs clear. Return the chiles to the bowl, cover with hot tap water, and place a heavy plate over the chiles to keep them submerged. Set aside to soak for another 30 minutes.

Drain the chiles and transfer to a blender along with the ground spices, roasted garlic, vinegar, salt, and 1 cup water; puree to a paste. Transfer to a container and refrigerate until ready to use.

BURNT JALAPEÑO POWDER

This riff on chilmole uses fresh green chiles instead of dried. Rather than rinsing off the char and mellowing it with additional aromatics as I would for chilmole, I simply grind the burnt jalapeños to a fine powder. The flavor is almost coffeelike, and it can be used to jack up the heat on anything from Black Bean Hummus Tacos (page 195) to a slice of pizza. Store it in an airtight container at room temperature for up to 1 month.

MAKES ABOUT 6 TABLESPOONS

10 jalapeño chiles, stemmed, seeded, and quartered lengthwise

Preheat the oven to 300°F. Arrange the chile quarters in an even layer on a baking sheet. Place the chiles in the oven and cook for about 3 hours, or until they are uniformly black and burnt; they will feel light and hollow.

Remove the chiles from the oven and let cool to room temperature. Working in batches, transfer the jalapeños to a spice grinder and grind to a fine powder. Transfer to a container and store at room temperature until ready to use.

COOKED BLACK AYOCOTE BEANS

Also called runner beans, these large specimens come in red, black, and white varieties. The ayocote's thick skin makes it a forgiving bean that isn't prone to bursting, and it has a meaty flavor that holds its own against other robust ingredients. Ayocotes make a silky puree for Black Bean Hummus Tacos (page 195), but they are also great served on their own as a side dish, simmered with pungent epazote and bay leaves. Store the cooked beans in the refrigerator in their own cooking liquid for up to 3 days.

MAKES ABOUT 5 CUPS, PLUS BEAN BROTH

2 cups dried black ayocote beans

1 medium white onion, halved

4 garlic cloves, peeled

2 dried bay leaves

1 epazote branch

Kosher salt, as needed

Sort through the beans and remove any stones or debris. Soak the beans in 3 quarts (12 cups) water for 12 hours or overnight.

Transfer the beans and their soaking liquid to a 6-quart stockpot over medium-high heat, along with the onion, garlic, bay leaves, and epazote. Bring to a simmer, then reduce the heat to medium and cook the beans gently until tender, about 90 minutes. (Do not skim.) If the waterline falls below the beans, top it off with more water to keep the beans submerged.

Remove the beans from the heat and let them cool to room temperature in their cooking liquid. Pick out the bay leaves, garlic cloves, and epazote and discard. Season to taste with salt. Transfer the beans in their cooking liquid to a container and refrigerate until ready to use.

COOKED WHITE BEANS

These delicate, creamy beans are used to add protein and heft to Mole Verde (page 86). Store the cooked beans in the refrigerator in their own cooking liquid for up to 3 days.

MAKES ABOUT 3 CUPS, PLUS BEAN BROTH

1 cup dried navy beans

1 medium white onion, halved

4 garlic cloves, peeled

1 handful dried avocado leaves

Kosher salt, as needed

Sort through the beans and remove any stones or debris. Soak the beans in 6 cups water for 12 hours or overnight.

Transfer the beans and their soaking liquid to a 6-quart stockpot over medium-high heat, along with the onion, garlic, and avocado leaves. Bring to a simmer, then reduce the heat to medium and cook the beans gently until tender, about 1 hour. (Do not skim.) If the waterline falls below the beans, top it off with more water to keep the beans submerged.

Remove the beans from the heat and let them cool to room temperature in their cooking liquid. Pick out the avocado leaves and garlic cloves and discard. Season to taste with salt. Transfer the beans in their cooking liquid to a container and refrigerate until ready to use.

GREEN CHORIZO

Chubby links of spiced sausages festoon the market stalls of Toluca, a Mexico City suburb and the chorizo capital of Latin America. You can find both red and green chorizo in Toluca—made with dried and fresh chiles, respectively. But the green links I've seen are always a suspect neon that suggests a heavy hand with food coloring. The vinegar in our version fades the hue to army green, and without any additives it doesn't look quite as splashy. But I find that the flavor of crumbly pork suffused with the tangy vinegar, serrano chiles, parsley, and spices is vivid enough on its own. The chorizo can be frozen in an airtight bag for up to 1 month.

MAKES ABOUT 1¼ POUNDS

1 pound ground pork

1 teaspoon black peppercorns

1 tablespoon coriander seeds

⅛ teaspoon cumin seeds

½ teaspoon dried Mexican oregano

1 dried bay leaf

4 whole cloves

8 garlic cloves, skins on

3 serrano chiles

¼ cup sherry vinegar

80 parsley leaves (from about 16 sprigs)

1 tablespoon kosher salt

Place the ground pork in a large bowl.

Set a 12-inch cast-iron skillet over medium heat for 5 minutes. Add the black peppercorns, coriander seeds, cumin seeds, oregano, bay leaf, and cloves; toast, shaking the pan, until fragrant, about 15 seconds. Remove from the heat, transfer to a spice grinder, and grind to a fine powder. Add to the bowl with the ground pork.

Reheat the skillet over medium heat. Add the garlic cloves and serrano chiles and roast, turning

recipe continues

them from time to time, until softened slightly and blackened in spots, about 6 minutes. Turn off the heat, remove the vegetables from the skillet, and set aside to cool at room temperature. Once they are cool enough to handle, peel the garlic cloves and discard the skins. Remove and discard the stems from the chiles.

Place the roasted garlic and serrano chiles in a blender along with the sherry vinegar, parsley, and salt, and puree until smooth. Transfer to the bowl with the ground pork and spices.

Mix the chorizo with your hands until thoroughly combined. Transfer to a container and refrigerate until ready to use.

RED CHORIZO

The same way that American chefs reach for bacon, I reach for red chorizo to add porky richness and dried chile depth to any number of dishes. The guajillos in this recipe give the sausage an almost fruity quality, balanced with fragrant spices and lots of roasted garlic. Red chorizo is enormously versatile, simple enough to make from scratch, and keeps well because of the vinegar content. You won't regret stowing a batch of this stuff in an airtight bag in your freezer for up to 1 month.

MAKES ABOUT 1½ POUNDS

1 pound ground pork

1 teaspoon black peppercorns

1 teaspoon coriander seeds

One 1-inch stick of canela (Mexican cinnamon)

1 tablespoon dried Mexican oregano

1 dried bay leaf

1 whole clove

10 guajillo chiles

10 garlic cloves, skins on

¼ cup cider vinegar

1 tablespoon kosher salt

2 tablespoons sugar

Place the ground pork in a large bowl.

Set a 12-inch cast-iron skillet over medium heat for 5 minutes. Add the peppercorns, coriander seeds, canela, oregano, bay leaf, and clove; toast, shaking the pan, until fragrant, about 15 seconds. Remove from the heat, transfer to a spice grinder, and grind to a fine powder. Add to the bowl with the ground pork.

Remove the stems from the guajillo chiles and tear the chiles open. Shake out and discard the seeds. Remove and discard the veins.

Reheat the skillet over medium heat. Toast the chiles, turning from time to time, until you see the first wisp of smoke, about 30 seconds. Transfer the chiles to a bowl, cover with hot tap water, and place a heavy plate over the chiles to keep them submerged. Set aside to soak for 30 minutes.

Add the garlic cloves to the skillet and roast, turning them from time to time, until softened slightly and blackened in spots, about 6 minutes. Turn off the heat, remove the garlic from the skillet, and set aside to cool at room temperature. Once they are cool enough to handle, peel the garlic cloves and discard the skins.

Drain the soaked chiles and discard the liquid. Place the chiles in a blender along with the roasted garlic, the vinegar, salt, and sugar, and puree until smooth. Transfer to the bowl with the ground pork and spices.

Mix the chorizo with your hands until thoroughly combined. Transfer to a container and refrigerate until ready to use.

BLOOD SAUSAGE

Mint and mezcal brighten the dense livery flavor that blood sausage is known for in this Oaxacan-inspired sangrita. Instead of piping the sausage into a casing and poaching it, I use a low-temperature oven to set the blood and bind the ground pork; I run a spoon through it once it is cool to get the crumbly texture that you'll want for the Fava and Blood Sausage Tacos (page 162).

You can buy pig's blood fresh or frozen at the butcher; the finished sausage will keep for up to 3 days in the refrigerator.

MAKES ABOUT 4½ CUPS

6 whole cloves

6 allspice berries

6 árbol chiles

¼ pound fatback, diced small

1 medium white onion, minced

1 tablespoon kosher salt

3 garlic cloves, minced

½ pound ground pork shoulder

1 dried bay leaf

40 mint leaves, chopped

2 cups pig's blood

¼ cup mezcal

¼ cup heavy cream

1 tablespoon vegetable oil

Preheat the oven to 200°F.

Set a 12-inch cast-iron skillet over medium heat for 5 minutes. Add the cloves and allspice berries and toast, shaking the pan, until fragrant, about 15 seconds. Remove from the heat, transfer to a spice grinder, and grind to a fine powder. Set aside in a bowl.

Place the skillet back over medium heat. Remove the stems from the árbol chiles and gently roll the chiles between your fingers to remove the seeds. Discard the seeds. Toast the chiles in the skillet, turning from time to time, until you see the first wisp of

recipe continues

smoke, about 30 seconds. Transfer the chiles to the spice grinder, grind to a fine powder, and add to the bowl with the ground spices.

Set a large sauté pan over medium heat. Add the fatback and cook until it begins to render, about 2 minutes. Add the onion and salt and cook, stirring, until the onion is translucent. Finally, add the garlic and cook until slightly softened, about 2 minutes.

Add the ground pork and bay leaf to the sauté pan and cook until the pork is crumbly, about 10 minutes. Remove from the heat and drain the excess fat into a heatproof bowl, leaving about 1 tablespoon in the pan. Let the mixture cool to room temperature.

Pick out the bay leaf and discard. Add the ground spices and chiles to the cooled pork, followed by the mint leaves. Transfer the mixture to a bowl and add the pig's blood, mezcal, and cream. Stir gently to combine.

Grease a 2-quart casserole with the vegetable oil. Pour the pork mixture into the dish in an even layer, cover with aluminum foil, and place on the top rack of the oven. Bake the blood sausage until it sets, about 45 minutes. Remove from the oven and let cool to room temperature. Run a spoon through the blood sausage to break it up, then transfer to a container and refrigerate until ready to use.

CHICKEN BROTH

Stocks and broths are a vital part of European cooking, but they aren't as common in the Mexican kitchen. When stocks do appear, they tend to be more diluted, with less of that concentrated meatiness you're typically aiming for. This is a simple stock recipe in that milder tradition, and it's a good one to have in your back pocket. Note that chicken stock is high in protein and low in acid, which means it's an ideal environment for bacteria to grow. You can rest the broth for a few minutes before straining to allow the particulates to settle, but then chill it pretty quickly to keep it in the safe zone. The stock will last up to 3 days in an airtight container in the refrigerator or up to 1 month in the freezer.

MAKES ABOUT 6½ CUPS

2 pounds chicken wings, necks, and backs

1 medium white onion, thinly sliced

2 carrots, peeled and diced

2 celery ribs, diced

2 dried bay leaves

2 garlic cloves, peeled

Rinse the chicken parts under cold running water and transfer to a 6-quart stockpot, along with the onion, carrots, celery, bay leaves, garlic, and 4 quarts water. Set over medium heat, bring to a simmer, then lower the heat so that the broth cooks gently. Cook for 6 hours, occasionally skimming any scum that accumulates on the surface of the broth. If the waterline falls below the chicken and vegetables, top it off with more water.

Remove the stockpot from the heat and let the broth rest for 20 minutes.

Set a fine-mesh sieve over a large bowl and ladle the broth through the strainer. Set the bowl into an ice bath to chill. When cooled to room temperature, transfer the broth to a container and refrigerate or freeze until ready to use.

SEAFOOD BROTH

Several recipes in this book call for fish, crab, or shrimp broth. Other than the protein, the recipes are identical, so I've given one master formula here.

For basic *fish* broth, use 2½ pounds of fish bones, rinsed of any residual blood and cut into 2-inch pieces. You can buy the bones frozen at many grocery stores, but fishmongers often sell them fresh by the pound. (Or simply save the bones from a lean fish dinner and use them to make stock. Flat fish are the best bet; avoid fatty fish like salmon or mackerel.) For *crab* broth, use 2 pounds of whole blue crabs, cut into quarters with a cleaver. *Shrimp* broth requires 2 pounds of shrimp, preferably with the heads on and shells intact, cut into 1-inch pieces. The broths will last up to 3 days in an airtight container in the refrigerator or up to 1 month in the freezer.

MAKES ABOUT 6½ CUPS

1 tablespoon vegetable oil

1 medium white onion, thinly sliced

Fish bones, blue crabs, or shrimp (see headnote)

2 dried bay leaves

2 garlic cloves, peeled

Set a 6-quart stockpot over medium heat and add the vegetable oil. Once the oil is shimmering, add the onion slices and sweat until translucent, stirring occasionally to prevent them from browning.

Add the fish, crab, or shrimp along with the bay leaves, garlic, and 2 quarts water. Bring to a simmer and cook for 30 minutes.

Remove the stockpot from the heat and let the broth rest for 20 minutes.

Set a fine-mesh sieve over a large bowl and ladle the broth through the strainer. Set the bowl into an ice bath to chill. When cooled to room temperature, transfer the broth to a container and refrigerate or freeze until ready to use.

PICKLED JALAPEÑOS

Simple pickled green chiles are an integral part of the recipe for Salsa Veracruz (page 73), but they are also a great way to add acid and extra heat to just about any taco. The pickled chiles will last up to 1 month in an airtight container in the refrigerator.

MAKES ABOUT 4 CUPS

6 jalapeño chiles, stemmed and quartered lengthwise

½ medium white onion, thinly sliced

2 garlic cloves, peeled

1 dried bay leaf

6 whole cloves

1 teaspoon allspice berries

2 cups cider vinegar

1 teaspoon kosher salt

6 tablespoons dark brown sugar

Place the jalapeños, onion, and garlic cloves in a nonreactive bowl.

Set a 12-inch cast-iron skillet over medium heat for 5 minutes. Add the bay leaf, cloves, and allspice, and toast, shaking the pan, until fragrant, about 15 seconds. Remove from the heat and transfer to the bowl with the jalapeños.

Set a small 1-quart saucepot over medium heat and add the vinegar, salt, and brown sugar. Bring to a simmer, then immediately remove from the heat and pour over the jalapeños.

Let the mixture cool to room temperature, then transfer to an airtight container and store in the refrigerator. Let the jalapeños pickle for at least 4 hours before using.

PICKLED RED ONIONS

These aromatic pickled onions are a must-have garnish for Cochinita Pibil Tacos (page 141). They will last up to 1 month in an airtight container in the refrigerator.

MAKES ABOUT 7 CUPS

4 medium red onions, thinly sliced

1 teaspoon black peppercorns

1 dried bay leaf

¼ teaspoon cumin seeds

1 tablespoon coriander seeds

2 cups cider vinegar

1 tablespoon kosher salt

1 tablespoon sugar

Place the onions in a nonreactive bowl.

Set a 12-inch cast-iron skillet over medium heat for 5 minutes. Add the peppercorns, bay leaf, cumin seeds, and coriander seeds; toast, shaking the pan, until fragrant, about 15 seconds. Remove from the heat and transfer to the bowl with the onions.

Set a small 1-quart saucepan over medium heat and add the vinegar, salt, and sugar. Bring to a simmer, then immediately remove from the heat and pour over the onions.

Let the mixture cool to room temperature, then transfer to an airtight container and store in the refrigerator. Let the onions pickle for at least 4 hours before using.

CREMA MEXICANA

Although sour cream is a common substitute, in Mexican culinary vernacular true *crema* is much closer to crème fraîche. It is lightly cultured and tangy, often with a pourable consistency. Because crema is a fermented product—it relies on the live cultures present in buttermilk or yogurt to encourage bacterial growth—you can safely store it in the refrigerator for a few weeks.

Crema can be used to thicken or enrich a dish, but it is broadly thought of as a condiment. If you're using it to garnish a taco, let it come to room temperature so that the crema can be drizzled on the taco.

MAKES ABOUT 2 CUPS

2 cups heavy cream

¼ cup cultured buttermilk

Set a small 1-quart saucepan over medium heat and add the cream. Cook the cream until it is just warm to the touch, about 2 minutes. Remove from the heat and pour into a container with a tight-fitting lid. Stir in the buttermilk and cover.

Let the cream ferment at room temperature for 48 hours. The crema will be slightly thickened with a pleasant, gently soured aroma. Store the crema in the refrigerator until ready to use.

NATAS

Making natas takes time and endurance. Scalding milk and harvesting the skin that forms on its surface over the course of several hours is the sort of cooking project you want to try when you have an afternoon to kill. You could buy clotted cream at the supermarket and save yourself the trouble, but no store-bought product compares to the natas you can make yourself—with just raw milk, heat, and patience. Good natas tastes clean and rich, with a texture that hovers somewhere between butter and whipped cream. Magnificent.

I find that it's easier to maneuver when working with a wide pan and a spoon with a flatter bottom, but the real key is to keep the milk at the right temperature—you want it just steaming so that it doesn't boil and agitate the skin. The first few collections tend to fall apart as you skim because they contain the most fat (the cream, as the saying goes, rises to the top). The natas will become sturdier as you continue to harvest. Also, note that you *must* obtain raw milk to make natas—the skin will not form if the milk is pasteurized and homogenized. You can store the finished natas in the refrigerator for up to 3 days.

MAKES ABOUT 2 CUPS

1 gallon raw (unpasteurized) cow's milk

Set a wide 5½-quart Dutch oven over medium heat and add the milk. Bring to a simmer, then turn down the heat so that the milk is just steaming, not bubbling. Cook at this temperature until a skin begins to form on the surface, about 15 minutes.

Using a tablespoon, carefully skim and remove the skin and collect it in a measuring cup.

Leave the milk scalding and undisturbed until another layer of skin forms, about 15 minutes. Carefully remove and collect. Continue to harvest the natas until you have collected about 2 cups—this will take about 6 hours. Note that as the milk continues to cook, the time between collections will shorten from 15 to about 10 minutes.

Transfer the natas to a container and refrigerate until ready to use.

RESOURCES

Where to find some of the specialized ingredients mentioned in this book.

ANSON MILLS
ansonmills.com
For: pickling lime (cal), rice, alternative flours

BOB'S RED MILL
bobsredmill.com
For: masa harina, alternative flours, beans, rice

BUONITALIA
buonitalia.com
For: lardo, capers

FRESH AND WILD
freshwild.com
For: dried chiles, chile pastes and powders, frozen huitlacoche, argan oil, black garlic, nuts and seeds, spices

HONEYVILLE
honeyville.com
For: dried white, yellow and blue whole-kernel corn, seeds, beans, alternative flours

KALUSTYAN'S
kalustyans.com
For: beans, dried whole-kernel corn, dried chiles, chile pastes and powders, spices, nuts and seeds, argan oil, olives

MASIENDA
masienda.com
For: multiple varieties of dried whole-kernel corn from small Mexican farms

MAST BROTHERS
mastbrothers.com
For: excellent South American and African chocolate

ROVEY SEED CO.
roveyseed.com
For: dried white, yellow and blue whole-kernel corn, pickling lime (cal)

TERRA SPICE
terraspice.com
For: dried chiles, achiote, avocado leaves, cocoa nibs, many whole spices

ACKNOWLEDGMENTS

FOR OUR BLOOD: Lauren Resler, Jaxon Stupak, Daniel Krieger, Al and Maryann Stupak, Debra and Glenn Rothman, Koke and Ron Portnoy, Torre Stupak, Mat Resler, Joshua, Hayyim, Esther, Kaddish and Sadira Rothman, Shirley Rauch, Ruth Krieger, Jane, Karen and Roz, Kevin and Laura Rice

FOR OUR COLLEAGUES AND COCONSPIRATORS: Kim Witherspoon and the Inkwell team, Francis Lam, Marysarah Quinn and everyone at Clarkson Potter, Evan Sung, Kaitlyn Du Ross, Diana Perez, Steve Sidman, David Markman

FOR OUR FOREBEARS AND FELLOW CHEFS: Rick Bayless, Diana Kennedy, Dave Arnold, Grant Achatz, Nick Kokonas, Ken Oringer, Wylie Dufresne, Enrique Olvera, Jorge Vallejo, Pedro Evia, Roberto Solis, Benito Molina and Solange Muris, Rosio Sánchez, Jordan Kahn, Chris Cosentino, Dave Chang, Christina Tosi

FOR OUR EMPELLÓN FAMILY: Seth Cohen, Amar Lalvani, David Rodolitz, Cory Lee, Isabel Coss, Hisham El-Wally, Jason Beberman, Aron "Narc" Pobereskin

FOR OUR FRIENDS, READERS AND CONFIDANTS: Kate Krader, Noah and Rae Bernamoff, Jacques and Hasty Torres, Michael and Heather Laiskonis, Maisie Wilhelm, Damian Higgins, Andrew Friedman, Allen Salkin, Kerry Diamond, Jennifer Mulak, Debra Drake, Jennifer Baum, Allyson Krieger, Bryan Campbell, Stephanie Nashban and Henry Asher, Chris Schonberger, Mari Uyehara, Daniel Gritzer, Julia Turshen, Charlotte Druckman, Alan Sytsma and Court Street Grocers, and the Harvard Club for letting us write our book in your hallowed halls

FOR OUR CATS: Percy, Lee, Charlotte, Birdie, and Mingus

INDEX

Note: Page references in *italics* indicate photographs.

ALEX STUPAK earned recognition as one of the world's most innovative pastry chefs while at Alinea and wd~50. His restaurant Empellón Cocina earned a James Beard nomination for the country's Best New Restaurant, and *Food & Wine* magazine named him a Best New Chef in 2013. He is the owner of Empellón Cocina, Empellón Taqueria, and Empellón al Pastor in New York City.

JORDANA ROTHMAN is a veteran food writer with credits that include *New York* magazine, *Food & Wine*, *Bon Appétit*, *Gastronomica*, and *Condé Nast Traveler*. The Food & Drink editor of *Time Out New York*, she was named one of the most influential icons on Twitter by *Time* in 2013.